THE
WISDOM OF BEN-SIRA

(ECCLESIASTICUS)

BY

W. O. E. OESTERLEY, D.D.

SOCIETY FOR PROMOTING
CHRISTIAN KNOWLEDGE
LONDON: 68, HAYMARKET, S.W.
1916

EDITORS' PREFACE

THE object of this series of translations is primarily to furnish students with short, cheap, and handy text-books, which, it is hoped, will facilitate the study of the particular texts in class under competent teachers. But it is also hoped that the volumes will be acceptable to the general reader who may be interested in the subjects with which they deal. It has been thought advisable, as a general rule, to restrict the notes and comments to a small compass; more especially as, in most cases, excellent works of a more elaborate character are available. Indeed, it is much to be desired that these translations may have the effect of inducing readers to study the larger works.

Our principal aim, in a word, is to make some difficult texts, important for the study of Christian origins, more generally accessible in faithful and scholarly translations.

In most cases these texts are not available in a cheap and handy form. In one or two cases texts have been included of books which are available in the official Apocrypha; but in every such case reasons exist for putting forth these texts in a new translation, with an Introduction, in this series.

W. O. E. OESTERLEY.
G. H. BOX.

THE WISDOM OF BEN-SIRA
(ECCLESIASTICUS)

INTRODUCTION

Title, Date, and Authorship

In most of the Greek manuscripts the title of our
book runs: "The Wisdom of Jesus, the son of
Sirach." This is presumably the translation of the
title in the original Hebrew; the proper names may,
however, be spelled in a way approximating more
closely to the original, thus: "The Wisdom of
Jeshua Ben-Sira." The title "Ecclesiasticus" comes
from the Old Latin Bible; it was the name by which
the book had been known to the Western Church
from the third century, and was, therefore, adopted
by St. Jerome when he made his Latin Version of
the Bible. The book was much used in the early
Church for instruction in conduct of life, especially
in the case of catechumens; it thus became the
ecclesiastical, or Church book, in a special sense;
this, in all probability, accounts for the title "Ecclesiasticus," so familiar to us. From the book itself
we gain two indications as to its date. In the
Prologue the writer's grandson speaks of himself
as "having come into Egypt in the eight and thirtieth
year of Euergetes the king." This Euergetes must
be the second of the name, as he was the only one who
reigned for over thirty-eight years; he was proclaimed
king at Alexandria in 170 B.C. The thirty-eighth
year of his reign would thus be 132 B.C. It was in

this year that the author's grandson, as he tells us, came into Egypt; and very soon after he made the Greek translation of his grandfather's Hebrew work. It is not unreasonable to assume that the translator's grandfather lived and worked some half century earlier than the time of his grandson; so that we may say that the original of our book was written, approximately, between the years 190–180 B.C. With this will, then, agree the other indication of date; in l. 1, mention is made of the high-priest Simon, the son of Onias (the Greek form of the Hebrew " Jochanan "), of whom the author writes in glowing terms when describing his ministerial service in the Temple. We know that a Simon II was high-priest in Jerusalem at the beginning of the second century B.C.; it is, therefore, fairly certain that it is to this Simon (Simon the Righteous, as he was called) that Ben-Sira is referring. This, therefore, also points to the first quarter of the second century B.C. as the approximate date of our book.

Nothing is known of the author beyond certain *data* to be gathered from his book; these are, however, interesting, and give us some clear ideas about him. Ben-Sira was a scribe and a teacher; his grandson, in the Prologue, says of him that he had devoted his life to the study of " the Law and the Prophets and the other books of our fathers," and was therefore induced to write something on his own account with the object of helping others " to make the more progress by a manner of life that is in accordance with the Law." Study of the Law and inculcating legal precepts constituted the essence of scribal activity. It is highly probable that in describing what he conceived to be the ideal scribe (xxxix. 1–3), Ben-Sira was, in the first instance, thinking of himself. But it must be remembered that Ben-Sira represents the older type of scribe, not the later Pharisaic scribe whose purview was more circumscribed and whose mental outlook was far narrower. It is the later type which we see portrayed in the Gospels. The older school of scribes, of which Ben-Sira was such an admirable representative, took a larger view of things; they did not restrict themselves to the purely legal aspect of the moral code; their ethical teaching was applied to all human activities; the scribe, that is to say, was also a *chacham* or " wise man," whose aim it was to show that wisdom, whether in the directly religious sense, or whether of a more worldly character, was a gift from God; and, as such, must be cultivated by every true Israelite in all its manifold forms. Ben-Sira tells us that for the purpose of teaching wisdom he had his *Beth ha-Midrash*, or " House of instruction," where he presumably gave lectures, and to which he invited all who needed instruction to come—

" Turn in unto me, ye unlearned,
And lodge in my house of instruction " (li. 23).

A few autobiographical notes are scattered about in the book. Thus it would seem from xxxix. 4 that Ben-Sira had spent some time in the service of an influential person, whether a Jew or a Gentile is uncertain; he also appears to have sojourned at the court of some foreign ruler. That he spent some considerable time in travel may be gathered both from the passage just referred to, and also from xxxiv. 12, li. 13. On one occasion he was in danger of his life, but was saved through his own wisdom (xxxiv. 13). He also tells us that he was once the victim of slander, with results that would have been very serious had it not been through Divine mercy which delivered him from the wiles of an enemy. Ben-Sira was a man with deep religious feeling; this comes out very clearly over and over again in his book; he combines real piety with robust common sense; his vivid belief in Divine providence is not permitted to obscure the intensely important part that man's free-will has to play. Moreover, he has a profound knowledge of human nature, its weaknesses and hypocrisies, but also its many excellencies; if there are some callings in life which he does not admire, he does not therefore deny their indispensableness; regarding others, *e. g.* that of the physician, he holds very exalted views; the physician, no less than the teacher and the priest, is God's minister; and he requires that man should recognize this. Ben-Sira was a truly admirable man, a real witness for God, and one who intensely desired to benefit his fellow-creatures; this, his life's work, was, as the ages testify, a glorious success.

General Character of the Book

Ecclesiasticus is a Moral Guide-Book to right living. It is a striking example of the Wisdom Literature. In one marked respect it shows an advance upon all previous examples of this literature which have come down to us; the writer is not content with giving a simple proverb, but he expands it by way of emphasizing its point and driving home its force; in the case of an obscure reference this is sometimes helpful; but, generally speaking, it does not enhance the value of what is written; a good proverb will often lose force by explanatory expansion, and its diverse application is in danger of restriction if the range of its content be circumscribed; and this seems not infrequently to be the case in our book.

Further, it is characteristic of the book that it presents the *Jewish* conception of Wisdom to the exclusion of every other. "In a sense," therefore, "Ecclesiasticus may be regarded as an apologetic work, inasmuch as it aims at combating the rising influence of Greek thought and culture among the Jews. Hellenism had already begun to affect the Jewish people, in Palestine as well as in the Dispersion, and here and there in the book one can observe that the writer himself, in spite of his conservatism, was not wholly unaffected by it. His travels had, no doubt, widened his mental horizon, and while he clings to the old he is, probably unconsciously, influenced by the new." [1] Speaking generally, however, it is true to say that the book represents, in contrast to the later Pharisaic attitude, the traditional Sadducæan religious standpoint.[2]

The Special Importance of the Book

Apart from subsidiary points, the special importance of the book from our present point of view lies (1) in the interesting details it contains concerning the social life and conditions of the Jews of Palestine during the two centuries immediately preceding the Christian era, and, more important still, (2) the insight it affords into the Jewish doctrinal teaching at this period.

(1) We have no other book which gives us such a clear glimpse of the social conditions, and of Jewish life generally of the period, as this does. The writer is so interested in men and their affairs, and so desirous of helping them with sound advice, that he is forced to lay bare their ways and manner of life in the very process of giving counsel and guidance. Thus, we get details of home life; the relations between husband and wife; between father and son; and father and daughter; between master and slave; between physician and patient; he tells of the doings of merchants, of hucksters; discusses the relationship between debtor and creditor; he has much to say on the subject of suretyship; he shows us something of high life, of dinner parties, and of musical entertainments; he inveighs against the evils of luxurious living; he deals with the subject of the rich and the poor. These, together with many other topics, give us a real insight into the conditions of human society which is of the greatest interest.

(2) As regards doctrinal teaching the book contains

[1] See the present writer's *Ecclesiasticus*, in the " Cambridge Bible for Schools," p. xxiv. (1912).

[2] This somewhat difficult subject is dealt with at length in the writer's *The Books of the Apocrypha : their origin, teaching and contents*, pp. 334–344 (1915).

a great deal which is of real importance for the study of the Gospels and of the New Testament as a whole. We get a thorough insight into the tenets of Judaism which throws much light on the teaching of our Lord, both from the point of view of its Jewish background, as well as its contrast to traditional Jewish teaching. One has but to mention such subjects as the doctrine of God, of the Law, the doctrine of Sin, of Atonement, of Grace and Free-will, of Works, the teaching on Worship, and the doctrine of the Future Life—with all of which our book is concerned—in order to realize how important and varied is the doctrinal teaching of the book, and therefore its great value in off ring us a detailed picture of the Jewish doctrinal background of the New Testament.

The Hebrew Manuscripts

A brief word must be said, in conclusion, about the recently found Hebrew manuscripts of Ecclesiasticus. At various times during the years 1896–1900 fragments of these manuscripts were brought to light and published; they all came ultimately from the Cairo *Genizah*.[1] The discovery and publication of the manuscripts is due to a number of scholars, viz. Mrs. Lewis, Mrs. Gibson, Sayce, Schechter, Cowley, Neubauer, Taylor, G. Margoliouth, Lévi, Adler, and Gaster. The fragments belong to four different Hebrew manuscripts; they cover nearly two-thirds of the whole book. The discovery of these manuscripts has given rise to some very intricate textual problems, especially when their relationship to the Greek and Syriac Versions is considered. Put briefly and generally the state of affairs seems to be something of this kind: " We must suppose

[1] *Genizah* is the name given to a room which adjoins many synagogues, and which is used for storing up disused manuscripts of books of the Bible. When rolls which have been used in the synagogue worship have become soiled or torn, they are not destroyed, but are hidden away in the *Genizah*; the word comes from a Hebrew root meaning " to hide."

an original Hebrew text; at different times various recensions of this came into existence; we know nothing of the history of these recensions, but apparently each recension possessed certain elements which were more faithful to the original text than the corresponding parts in the others. The Greek and Syriac Versions were made from different recensions, which would account for the fact that the Greek and the Syriac have each preserved certain original elements not possessed by the other. Our present Hebrew text represents yet another recension, but has suffered a great deal in transmission, and it too, therefore, contains elements of its own not possessed by the Greek and Syriac Versions. Though the task is very difficult, and sometimes impossible, yet in seeking to reconstruct, whenever feasible, the original Hebrew, the Greek and Syriac texts are indispensable, seeing that they contain many passages which represent a better Hebrew text than that of our Hebrew manuscripts; while these, again, in other passages, presuppose an underlying Hebrew text which is purer than those of either the Greek or the Syriac." [1] Taken as a whole, the text of the Hebrew manuscripts comes, of course, much nearer to the original form of our book than the Greek and Syriac translations; their discovery has, therefore, rendered our Revised Version, so far as this book is concerned, to a very great extent antiquated.

Bibliography

For editions of the Hebrew, Greek, Old Latin, and Syriac texts, and critical discussions on these, see Box and Oesterley in Charles' *The Apocrypha and Pseudepigrapha of the Old Testament*, vol. i. pp. 314, 315 (1913).

Commentaries by foreign scholars are those of Fritzsche (1859), Ryssel (1900), Knabenbauer (1902), Peters (1902), Strack (1903), Lévi (1904), and Smend

[1] See the present writer's *Ecclesiasticus* (Cambridge Bible), pp. xciv., xcv.

(1906). English Commentaries are those of Edersheim, in Wace's *Apocrypha*, vol. i. (1888), Oesterley, in the Cambridge Bible (1912), Box and Oesterley, in Charles' *Apocrypha and Pseudepigrapha of the Old Testament*, vol. i. (1913).

In the following translation Smend's Hebrew text is taken as a basis wherever the Hebrew is extant; otherwise Swete's Greek text has been followed. On the outer margin it is indicated from which of these two the translation is made, so that the reader can see at once if he is reading from the Hebrew or the Greek. Only important variants and emendations are given in the foot-notes. Where the Greek text (the Hebrew not being extant) is inferior to the Syriac, the latter is given in the foot-notes. It has not been thought necessary to indicate in the foot-notes obvious corrections of orthographical errors in the Hebrew text.

References to Old Testament quotations, etc., have only been given in a few special cases, as in the case of Ecclesiasticus these are so numerous that if they were all noted the text would be overloaded with little figures referring to foot-notes.

The titles to the various sections are not, as a rule, part of the text; in the few instances in which this is the case the fact is noted in the foot-notes. Explanatory notes are given as rarely as possible; for the explanation of difficult passages readers must consult one or more of the Commentaries mentioned above.

[. . . .] = something supplied which is implied, though not expressed, in the original, in order to make the translation clearer.

[. . . .] = verses which are later insertions not found in the best Greek manuscripts; with one exception (xvi. 15, 16) these never occur in the Hebrew.

(?) = an uncertain reading owing to a mutilation of the Hebrew text.

G = *Grk.*, H = *Heb.*, L = *Lat.*, S = Syr.

THE WISDOM OF SIRACH

PROLOGUE

FORASMUCH as many and great things have been
delivered unto us through the Law and the Prophets
and the others that followed after them (for the which
praise is due to Israel for instruction and wisdom),
moreover, since not only should the readers themselves become proficient in these, but such lovers of
learning should be able both by speaking and writing
to profit them that are without,—my grandfather
Jesus, having given himself greatly to the reading
of the Law and the Prophets and the other books of
our fathers, and having acquired sufficient familiarity
in them, was also himself led to take a part in writing
something appertaining to instruction and wisdom,
in order that those who are lovers of learning and
instructed in these things might make so much the
more progress by a manner of life that is in accordance with the Law. Ye are, therefore, entreated
to undertake the reading [of this book] with kindli-
ness and attentiveness, and to be indulgent if in any
parts of what we have laboured to interpret we seem
to fall short in [the rendering of] some of the phrases.
For when things spoken in Hebrew are translated
into another tongue they have not quite the same
meaning; and not only these things [which follow]
but the Law itself, and the Prophecies, and the rest
of the books, convey a different meaning when
spoken in their original [language]. Now in the
thirty-eighth year under king Euergetes, having
come into Egypt, and remained there, I found

opportunity[1] of [imparting] no small amount of instruction. I, therefore, considered it altogether incumbent upon me to devote some zeal and love-labour to [the task of] interpreting this book; devoting, in truth, much sleepless care and skill in the interval in order to publish it—having brought the book to an end—also for those who in the land of their sojourning desire to be lovers of learning, being already predisposed, in regard to their ethical culture, to live in accordance with the Law.

I. 1–10. The Origin of Wisdom

G   1. All wisdom is from the Lord,
        And is with Him for ever.
    2. The sand of the seas, and the rain-drops,
        And the days of eternity,—who can number them?
    3. The height of heaven, and breadth of earth,
        And the deep,[2]—who can trace out?
    4. Wisdom was created before all,
        And wise insight from everlasting.
    [5. The source of Wisdom is the word of God in the heights,
        And her ways are eternal commandments.]
    6. To whom hath the root of Wisdom been revealed?
        And who hath discerned her subtleties?
    [7. To whom hath the understanding of Wisdom been manifested?
        And who hath grasped her rich experience?]
    8. One there is Who is wise, greatly to be feared,
        The Lord sitting upon His throne;
    9. He Himself created her, and saw, and numbered her,
        And poured her out upon all His works;

---

[1] This represents the reading of a few unimportant Greek MSS., but it gives the best sense, and has therefore been adopted.

[2] *Grk.* adds " and wisdom "; *Syr. Lat.* omit.

G

10. In measure [1] upon all flesh,
  But without measure doth He grant her to
  them that love Him.

I. 11–20. The Fear of the Lord

11. The fear of the Lord is glory and exultation,
  And gladness and a crown of joy.
12. The fear of the Lord delighteth the heart,
  And giveth gladness, and joy, and length of
  days.
13. For him that feareth the Lord it shall be well at
  the last,
  And in the day of his death he shall find grace.
14. The beginning of Wisdom is to fear God,
  And with the faithful was she created in the
  womb;
15. And he hath established [2] her foundation among
  men for ever,
  And with their seed shall she be had in trust. [3]
16. To fear the Lord is the fulness of Wisdom,
  And she intoxicateth them with her fruits.
17. She filleth all her house with desirable things,
  And her garners with the things she bringeth
  forth.
18. A crown of Wisdom is the fear of the Lord,
  Making peace to flourish and healthful healing.
19. And He saw and numbered her, and rained down
  insight and wise discernment, [4]
  And exalted the glory of them that hold her
  fast.
20. To fear the Lord is the root of Wisdom,
  And her branches are length of days.
[21. The fear of the Lord driveth away sins,
  And he who abideth therein will avert all
  wrath.]

[1] *Lit.* " according to His gift."
[2] *Lit.* " she hath nested."
[3] The text of verse 15 is uncertain.
[4] The text of this line is out of order; *Syr.*, which is to be
preferred, reads:
  " She is a strong staff and a glorious stay."

G   I. 22–30.   **The Exercise of Wisdom**

22. Unrighteous wrath cannot be justified,
    For the wrath [1] of his anger will [occasion] his
        fall.
23. The longsuffering man endureth until the [proper]
        time,
    And in the end joy will arise for him;
24. He suppresseth [2] his words until the [proper]
        time,
    And the lips of the faithful [3] will declare his
        understanding.
25. In the treasures of Wisdom there is a wise
        proverb,[4]
    But godliness is an abomination to the sinner.
26. If thou desire Wisdom keep the commandments,
    And the Lord will grant her freely unto thee.
27. For the fear of the Lord is wisdom and instruction,
    And faith and meekness are well-pleasing unto
        Him.[5]
28. Disobey not the fear of the Lord,
    And come not nigh thereto with a double
        heart.
29. Be not a hypocrite in the sight [6] of men,
    And take heed to [the utterances of] thy lips.
30. Exalt not thyself lest thou fall
    And bring upon thyself disgrace,
    And the Lord reveal thy hidden [thoughts],
    And cast thee down in the midst of the assembly,
    Because thou camest not unto the fear of the
        Lord,
    And thy heart was full of deceit.

[1] So א *Lat.*; all other *Grk.* MSS. read " sway."
[2] *Lit.* " hideth."
[3] אA read " many."
[4] Some *Grk.* MSS. read " proverbs."
[5] *Lit.* " His good pleasure."
[6] So *Syr. Lat.* and one *Grk.* cursive; all other *Grk.* MSS.
read " in the mouths "; the error is due to a misreading of
the original Hebrew.

II. 1-6. **On Serving the Lord**

1. My son, when thou comest to serve the Lord **G.** God,
   Prepare thy soul for temptation.
2. Direct thy heart aright, and continue steadfast,
   And be not fearful [1] in time of calamity.
3. Cleave unto Him, and depart not [from Him],
   That thou mayest be increased at thy latter end.
4. Accept whatsoever is brought upon thee,
   And endure in the changes of thy humiliation; [2]
5. For gold is proved in the fire,
   And acceptable men in the furnace of humiliation.
6. Trust in Him and He will help thee,
   Make straight thy ways and hope in Him.

II. 7-11. **They that fear the Lord are blessed**

7. Ye that fear the Lord, wait for His mercy;
   And turn not aside lest ye fall.
8. Ye that fear the Lord, put your trust in Him,
   And your reward shall not fail.
9. Ye that fear the Lord, hope for good things,
   And for eternal gladness and mercy.
10. Regard the generations of old, and see:
    Who ever trusted in the Lord, and was put
    . to shame?
    Or who did abide in His fear, and was forsaken?
    Or who called on Him, and was overlooked?
11. For the Lord is compassionate and merciful,
    And forgiveth sins, and saveth in time of trouble.

II. 12-14. **Woe unto the Faithless**

12. Woe unto fearful hearts and faint hands,
    And to the sinner that goeth two ways.

---

[1] *Lit.* " haste not."
[2] *Syr.* " And be patient in disease and poverty."

B

G. 13. Woe unto the faint heart; because it believeth not,

Therefore it shall not be sheltered.

14. Woe unto you that have lost patience,

And what will ye do when the Lord visiteth you?

II. 15–18. **They that fear the Lord**

15. They that fear the Lord will not be disobedient to His words,

And they that love Him will keep His ways.

16. They that fear the Lord will seek His good pleasure,

And they that love Him will be filled with the Law.

17. They that fear the Lord will make ready their hearts,

And will humble themselves in His sight.

18. Let us fall into the hands of the Lord,

And not into the hands of men.[1]

For as is His majesty, so also is His mercy,

S. And as is His name, so also are His works.[2]

III. 1–16. **Filial Duty and its Reward**

S. L. 1. Hearken, ye children, unto the judgement of your father,[3]

G. And act accordingly that ye may be saved.

2. For the Lord hath given the father glory as touching the children,

And hath established the judgement of the mother as touching the sons.

3. He that honoureth [his] father maketh atonement for sins,

4. And he that giveth glory to his mother is as one that layeth up treasure.

---

[1] The two first lines of verse 18 have got out of place, they are wanting in *Syr.*

[2] This line has fallen out in *Grk.* (see note on vi. 17).

[3] The *Grk.* text is corrupt here.

5. He that honoureth [his] father shall have joy of **G.**
    [his] children,
  And he that giveth glory to his mother is as one
    that layeth up treasure.[1]
  And in the day of his prayer he shall be heard.
6. He that giveth glory to [his] father shall have
    length of days,
  And he that obeyeth the Lord giveth rest to
    his mother.[2]
7. He that feareth the Lord honoureth his father,
  And serveth his parents as masters.[3]
8. My son, in word and deed honour thy father,   **H.**
  In order that every blessing may come upon
    thee.
9. The blessing of a father maketh firm the root,
  But the curse of a mother rooteth up the young
    plant.
10. Exult not in the dishonour of thy father,
  For it is no glory to thee.
11. A man's glory is his father's glory,
  And he that dishonoureth his mother multi-
    plieth sin.
12. My son, be strong in the glory of thy father,[4]
  And grieve him not all the days of his life;
13. Yea, and if his mind fail, be considerate with
    him,
  And dishonour him not all the days of his life.
14. Alms [given] to a father shall not be blotted out,
  And it shall stand firm as a substitute for sin.
15. In the day of trouble it shall be remembered [for
    thy benefit],
  Obliterating thine iniquities as heat the hoar-
    frost.

[1] This line has been inadvertently repeated from verse 4; it is omitted by all the *Grk.* MSS. with the exception of B.
[2] *Syr.* " And he that giveth rest to his mother shall receive his reward from God "; this is to be preferred.
[3] The text of verse 7 is corrupt, the rendering given above is that of *Lat.* and three *Grk.* cursives.
[4] *Grk.* " My son, help thy father in his old age "; this is to be preferred.

H. 16. As one that is arrogant is he that despiseth his
     father,
        And as one that provoketh his Creator is he
        that curseth his mother.

III. 17–25. **Humility**

17. My son, when in prosperity walk humbly,
       And thou wilt be loved more than the giver
       of gifts.
18. Be meek when thou art exalted,[1]
       And thou wilt find mercy in the sight of God.
G. [19. Many are exalted and esteemed,
       But the mysteries ⌐of God] are revealed to the
       lowly.]
H. 20. For many are the mercies of God,
       And He revealeth His secret to the humble.
21. Enquire not into that which is too wonderful for
    thee,
       And search not for that which is hidden from
       thee.
22. Meditate upon what thou hast power [to under-
    stand],
       And meddle not with that which is hid.
23. With that which is beyond [thee] have nought
    to do,
       For more than thou understandest hath been
       shown thee.
24. For many are the thoughts of the sons of men,
       And evil imaginations lead astray.
25. Where no apple of the eye is light faileth,
       And where no knowledge is wisdom faileth.

III. 26–31. **Men reap what they sow**

26. A stubborn heart suffereth evil at its latter end,
       But he that loveth the things that are good
       shall be brought unto them.
27. A stubborn heart,—many are its troubles,
       And the profane man addeth iniquity to
       iniquity.

[1] *Lit.* " Make small thy soul in all greatness."

28. There is no healing for the wound of him that is a **H.**
     scorner,
     For an evil plant is his plant.
29. A wise heart discerneth the proverbs of the
     wise,
     And the ear that listeneth to wisdom rejoiceth.
30. A flaming fire doth water quench,
     So doth almsgiving atone for sin.
31. He that doeth good, it shall meet him in his
     ways,
     And when he falleth he shall find a stay.

IV. 1–10. Kindness to the Poor and Afflicted

1. My son, mock not at the life of the poor,
    And grieve not the eyes of the bitter in
    spirit.
2. The soul that is in want cause not to sigh,
    And vex not the heart of the oppressed.
3. The inward parts of the poor grieve not,
    And withhold not a gift from the afflicted.
4. Despise not the supplication of the poor,
    And turn thyself not from the broken in spirit.
5. From him that asketh turn not away thine **G.**
    eye,[1]
    And give him no cause to curse thee.   **H.**
6. When the bitter in spirit crieth in the anguish of
    his soul,
    His Rock [2] hearkeneth unto the voice of his
    cry.
7. Make thyself beloved in the assembly,
    And bow thy head to the city elders.
8. Incline thine ear to the afflicted,
    And respond to his greeting with humility.
9. Save the oppressed from his oppressors,
    And let not thy spirit show contempt in a
    righteous cause.

[1] The *Heb.* is wanting here.
[2] *Grk.* reads : " He that formed him " ; this reading is to be
preferred.

H. 10. Be as a father to orphans,
        And in place of a husband to widows;
        Then God will call thee His son,
        And be gracious unto thee and save thee from
            destruction.[1]

IV. 11-19. **The Reward of those who seek Wisdom**

11. Wisdom teacheth her children,
        And taketh hold of all that give heed to her.
12. They that love her love life,
        And they that seek her shall obtain grace from
            the Lord.
13. They that take hold of her shall find glory from
            the Lord,
        And they shall abide in the glory of the Lord.
14. They that serve her serve the Holy One,
        And God loveth them that love her.
15. He that hearkeneth unto me shall judge in truth,
        And he that giveth ear unto me shall dwell in
            my innermost chamber.
G. 16. If thou trust her thou shalt inherit her,
        And his generations shall be in possession [of
            her].[2]
H. 17. For I will disguise myself and walk with him,
        And at first I will try him with temptations.
G.   Fear and dread will she [3] bring upon him,[4]
H.   And I will chastise him with scourges,
        Until his heart is filled with me,
G.   And she will try him with her ordinances.[5]

---

[1] *Lit.* " The Pit."
[2] Verse 16 is not extant in *Heb.* The rendering of *Syr.*, which is to be preferred, runs:

" If he trust me he shall inherit me,
    And he shall possess me on behalf of all the generations of
        the age."

[3] *Syr.* reads " I."
[4] This line is not extant in *Heb.*
[5] This line does not occur in *Heb.* or *Syr.*; it is probably a gloss.

18. [Then] will I lead him on again,
    And will reveal to him my hidden things.
19. If he turn [from me] I will forsake him,
    And deliver him to the spoilers.

H.

IV. 20–31. **Words of Guidance**

20. My son, observe times and seasons, and fear evil,
    And concerning thyself be not ashamed.
21. For there is a shame that bringeth iniquity,
    And there is a shame [that bringeth] glory and grace.
22. Respect no man to thine own hurt,
    And be not ashamed [when it is] to thy stumbling.
23. Withhold not a word in season,
    And hide not thy wisdom;
24. For by speech is Wisdom known,
    And understanding by the tongue's utterance.
25. Speak not against God,
    But be humble towards God.
26. Be not ashamed to confess sin,
    And stand not against the stream.
27. Do not humiliate thyself in the presence of a fool,
    And show no respect to the oppressor.
28. Strive for the right until death,
    And the Lord will fight for thee.
29. Be not boastful with thy tongue,
    [Nor] careless or negligent in thy work.
30. Be not like a lion in thine house,
    Nor tyrannous or terrible to thy servants.
31. Let not thy hand be stretched out to take,
    And closed in the time of giving back.

V. 1–3. **Wealth is a False Security**

1. Trust not in thy wealth,
    And say not, " I have power."

H. 2. Trust not in thy wealth,[1]
       To walk after the desire of thy soul.[1]
       Go not after [the desire of] thine heart and of
          thine eyes,
       To walk after the desires of thy soul.
    3. Say not, " Who hath power over me ? "
       For the Lord avengeth the persecuted.

V. 4-8. Divine Mercy and Justice

    4. Say not, " I sinned, and what happened unto
          me ! "
       For the Lord is longsuffering.
    5. Count not upon forgiveness,
       By adding sin to sin.
    6. And say not, " His mercies are great,
       He will forgive the multitude of my sins ; "
       For mercy and wrath are with Him,
       And upon the wicked doth His anger abide.
    7. Delay not to turn unto Him,
       And put it not off from day to day ;
       For suddenly doth His indignation come forth,
       And in the time of vengeance thou wilt perish.
    8. Trust not in unrighteous gains,
       For they profit nothing in the day of wrath.

V. 9—VI. 1. The Bridling of the Tongue

    9. Winnow not with every wind,
       And walk not in every path.
   10. Be steadfast in regard to thy knowledge,
       And let thy speech be consistent.
   11. Be swift in hearing,
       But slow in replying.
   12. If thou canst, answer thy neighbour,
       But if not,—hand on mouth !
   13. Glory and dishonour come through speaking,
       And the tongue of a man [bringeth] his fall.

---

[1] These two lines are obviously doublets; they are omitted
in *Grk.*; *Syr.* has the first and last lines of the verse.

H.

14. Be not called " Master Two-tongues " ;
    And slander not with thy tongue ;
    Because for the thief hath shame been created,
    And sore reproach for " Master Two-tongues."
15. [Be it] a small or a great matter deal not corruptly
        [therein] ;
VI. 1. And be not an enemy in place of a friend,
    An evil name, reproach, and shame wouldest thou
        get,
        [For] thus it is with the evil man, " Master
    Two-tongues."

VI. 2-4. Self-control

2. Fall not into the power of thy soul,[1]
    Lest thou consume thy strength.
3. It will devour thy leaf and destroy thy fruit,
4.   And will leave thee as a dried-up tree.
    For unbridled passion destroyeth the possessor
        thereof.
    And maketh him the joy of his enemy.

VI. 5-17. Friendship, true and false

5. Kindly speech maketh many friends,
    And gracious lips [multiply] those that give
        greeting.
6. Let those that are at peace with thee be many,
    But thy confidant one in a thousand.
7. When thou makest a friend test him,[2]
    And be in no hurry to trust him.
8. For there is a friend who is a time-server,
    And he continueth not in the day of trouble.
9. And there is a friend who is turned into an enemy,
    And he revealeth strife to thy reproach.[3]
10. And there is a friend who is a table-friend,
    Who is not to be found in the evil day ;

---

[1] *I. e.* Be not a slave to thy passions.
[2] *Lit.* " Acquire him by testing."
[3] See Prov. xxv. 9, 10.

H. 11. In thy prosperity he will be like thee,
    And will lord it over thy servants; [1]

   12. [But] if evil overtake thee he will turn against thee,
    And will hide himself from thee.

   13. Separate thyself from thine enemies,
    And as to thy friends be on thy guard.

   14. A faithful friend is a strong defence,
    And he that findeth such findeth a treasure.

   15. A faithful friend is beyond price,
    And there is no weighing of his goodness.

   16. " A bundle of life " [2] is a faithful friend,
    He that feareth God obtaineth him.

G. 17. He that feareth the Lord directeth his friendship aright,[3]

H.   And as he is, so is his friend.

VI. 18–37. The Search for Wisdom

G. 18. [My] son, from thy youth up choose instruction,
    And thou wilt find Wisdom even unto [the time of] grey hairs.[4]

H. 19. As the ploughman and the reaper draw thou nigh unto her,
    And hope for the abundance of her fruits.
   For in cultivating her thou toilest but a little,
    And to-morrow thou shalt eat her fruits.

   20. She is harsh to the fool,
    And he that lacketh understanding abideth not in her;

   21. Like a burdensome stone is she upon him,
    And he is not slow in casting her off.

   22. For [as to] Wisdom, as her name so is she,
    And not to many is she clear.

G. 23. Hearken, [my] son, and receive my judgement,
    And refuse not my counsel; [5]

---

[1] Amended text, on the basis of *Grk.*; the *Heb.* text is corrupt.
   [2] See 1 Sam. xxv. 29.   [3] This line is missing in *Heb.*
   [4] Verse 18 is missing in *Heb.*
   [5] Verses 23, 24, 26 are not extant in *Heb.*

24. And bring thy feet into her fetters,   **G.**
    And into her chain thy neck.[1]
25. Bow down thy shoulder and bear her,   **H.**
    And chafe not under her bonds.
26. With all thy soul draw nigh unto her,   **G.**
    And with all thy might observe her paths.[1]
27. Enquire and search, seek and find,   **H.**
    And take hold of her, and let not go of her;
28. For at last thou wilt find her rest,
    And she will be turned into delight for thee;
29. And her net will become for thee a stay of
      strength,
    And her bonds robes of gold.
30. An ornament of gold is her yoke,
    And her fetters a cord of blue.[2]
31. With glorious garments shalt thou array thyself,
    And with a crown of beauty shalt thou crown
      thyself with her.
32. If thou so desirest, my son, thou shalt become
      wise,
    And if thou settest thy heart [thereon] thou
      shalt become prudent.
33. If thou desire to bear, thou shalt receive,
    And if thou incline thine ear, thou shalt be
      wise.
34. Among the multitude of elders stand thou,   **G.**
    And whosoever is wise, cleave unto him.[3]
35. Desire to hear every discourse,   **H.**
    And the wise proverb, let it not escape thee.
36. Look for him who is wise, yea, search him out
      diligently,
    And let thy foot wear out his threshold.
37. Ponder the fear of the Most High,
    And of His commandments think continually;
    And He will make wise thy heart,
    And give thee wisdom in whatsoever thou
      desirest.

[1] Verses 23, 24, 26 are not extant in *Heb.*
[2] See Num. xv. 38.
[3] Verse 34 is not extant in *Heb.*

VII. 1-3. **Avoidance of Sin**

H. 1. Do no evil, then shall no evil come upon thee;
2.   Go far from iniquity, and it will turn from thee.
3. Sow not in the furrows of unrighteousness,[1]
Lest thou reap it sevenfold.

VII. 4-7. **Humility**

4. Seek not dominion from God,
Nor from a king a seat of honour.
5. Justify thyself not in the sight of God,
And affect not wisdom in the presence of a king.
6. Seek not to be a ruler,
Lest thou be not able to suppress presumption,
And thou be afraid in the presence of the mighty,
And [thus] put a stumbling-block in [the way of] thine integrity.
7. Be not a cause of evil in the assembly in the gate,
That thou be not cast down in the midst of the congregation.

VII. 8-10. **Vain Oblations**

8. Do not wickedly repeat a sin,
For of the first thou art [still] guilty.
G. 9. Say not, " He will look upon the multitude of my gifts,
And when I offer [them] to God Most High He will accept [them]." [2]
H. 10. Be not wearied in prayer,
And be not behindhand in almsgiving.

VII. 11-17. **Right Conduct of Life**

11. Despise no man [who is] in bitterness of spirit,
Remember there is One Who exalteth and humbleth.
12. Devise not violence against a brother,
Nor against a friend or companion withal.

---

[1] Emended text.   [2] Verse 9 is not extant in *Heb.*

13. Delight in no lie whatsoever,   H.
     For its consequence will not be pleasant.
14. Chatter not in the assembly of princes,
     And repeat not thy words in prayer.
15. Hate not laborious work,
     Nor husbandry, for it was ordained of God.[1]
16. Reckon not thyself among the sinful,
     Remember that wrath will not tarry.
17. Humble altogether [thy] pride,
     For the hope of man is worms.
     Hasten not to say, " [there is] violence ; " [2]
       Commit [thyself] unto God, and delight [in]
         His way.[2]

VII. 18-36. **Duties to All**

18. Change not a friend for money,
     Nor a natural brother for gold of Ophir.
19. Despise not a wise wife,
     And a comely one is above pearls.
20. Maltreat not a servant that serveth faithfully,
     Nor a hireling who giveth himself [for thee].
21. Love a wise servant as thine own self,
     And deny him not his freedom.
22. Art thou possessed of a beast of burden look after
       [it] thyself,
     And if it is a reliable [beast] retain possession
       [of it].
23. If thou hast sons, correct them,
     And give them wives in their youth.
24. If thou hast daughters keep their bodies [pure],
     And be not indulgent to them.[3]
25. Get thy daughter married, and worry will vanish,
     But bestow her on a sensible man.
26. If thou hast a wife abhor her not,
     But one that hateth thee trust not.

---

[1] The text of this line is corrupt.
[2] The text of these lines is corrupt; they are omitted in
Grk. Lat.
[3] *Lit.* " Cause not thy face to shine unto them."

G. 27. With thy whole heart honour thy father
　　　And forget not thy mother who bore thee in
　　　　travail.[1]

　28. Remember that through them thou wast begotten,
　　　And how canst thou recompense them for
　　　　[what they have done for] thee? [1]

H. 29. With all thy heart fear God,
　　　And reverence His priests.

　30. With all thy strength love Him that made thee,
　　　And forsake not His ministers.

　31. Glorify God, and honour [His] priest,
　　　And give [them] their portion as thou art
　　　　commanded,
　　　The food of the trespass-offering, and the heave-
　　　　offering of the hand,[2]
　　　The sacrifices of righteousness, and the offerings
　　　　of holy things.

　32. And also to the poor stretch forth thine hand,
　　　That thy blessing may be full.

　33. Acceptable is a gift to every living man,
　　　And also from the dead withhold not kindness.

　34. Shun not the sorrowful,
　　　And mourn with the mourners.

　35. Omit not to visit the sick,
　　　Because for this thou wilt be loved.

　36. In all thy doings remember thy latter end,
　　　Then wilt thou never act basely.

VIII. 1-3. Against Quarrelling

　1. Quarrel not with a powerful man,
　　　That thou fall not into his hands.
　　　That thou cause not his heart to turn,[3]
　　　　Quarrel not with one stronger than thou
　　　　　art.[3]

---

[1] Verses 27, 28 are not extant in *Heb*.
[2] See Exod. xxix. 27.
[3] These lines form a doublet and do not belong to the
original text.

2. Strive not against a rich man, **H.**
   Lest he "weigh thy price," and thou be
   destroyed.
   For gold hath made many reckless,
   And wealth hath led astray the hearts of princes.
3. Quarrel not with a loud-tongued man,
   And lay not wood on fire.

VIII. 4–19. Precepts for Right Conduct

4. Bandy not words with a fool
   Lest he despise thy sound words (?).
5. Humiliate not a man that repenteth,
   Remember that we all are guilty.
6. Dishonour not an aged man,
   For of us [there are] some [that] will grow **G.**
   old.[1]
7. Exult not over one that is dead, **H.**
   Remember that we all shall be gathered [to
   our fathers].
8. Neglect not the discourse of the wise,
   And occupy thyself with [their] deep sayings;
   For from these thou wilt gain instruction,
   So that they mayest stand in the presence of
   princes.
9. Reject not the tradition of the aged,
   Which they heard from their fathers;
   For thou wilt receive instruction from this,
   And [be able to] answer in time of perplexity.
10. Kindle not with the coals of the wicked,
    Lest thou be burned in the flame of his fire.
11. Lose not thy temper because of a scorner,
    So that he use thy mouth as a trap.
12. Lend not to a man that is wealthier than thou;
    If thou lend thou art [already] as one that
    loseth.
13. Go not surety for a better man than thou;
    If thou go surety thou art [already] as one that
    payeth.

---

[1] The text of *Heb.* is mutilated.

H. 14. Go not to law with a judge,
       For he will judge to his own advantage.
   15. Consort not with a cruel man,
       Lest thou load thyself with evil;
       For he will go according to his own bent,
       And through his folly thou wilt come to grief.
   16. Withstand not a wrathful man,
       And ride not with him in the way;
       For a light thing in his eyes is [the shedding of]
         blood,
       And where there is none to help he will destroy
         thee.
   17. With a simpleton take no counsel,
       For he cannot help thy secret.
   18. Before a stranger do nothing secret,
       For thou knowest not what he will ultimately
         do [therewith].
   19. Open not thy heart to every man,
       And drive not away [thus] thine own advantage.

IX. 1–9. Conduct towards Women

   1. Be not jealous of the wife of thy bosom,
      That she learn not bitterness against thee.
   2. Give not thyself unto a woman
      That she lord it not over thee.[1]
   3. Draw not nigh unto a strange woman,
      Lest thou fall by her entanglements.
      Consort not with an harlot,[2]
      Lest thou be caught in her snares.[2]
   4. Consort not with a female musician,
      Lest thou be taken in her snares.
   5. Gaze not on a maiden,
      Lest thou be ensnared in her penalties (?).
   6 Give not thyself to a harlot,
      Lest thou lose thine inheritance.

----

[1] *Lit.* " To cause her to tread upon thy high places," cf.
Hab. iii. 19.
[2] These lines form a doublet to verse 4, and do not belong
to the original text.

7. Look not around in the streets of the city,[1]   G.
   And wander not in the broad places thereof.   H.
8. Turn away thine eye from a beautiful woman,
   And gaze not upon beauty that belongeth not
      to thee;
   By the beauty of woman many have been ruined,
   For thus passion kindleth like a fire.
9. In the presence of a married woman lean not on
      thine elbow,
   And mingle not strong drink with her (?);
   Lest thou incline thine heart unto her,
   And in thy blood goest down to the Pit.

IX. 10–16. Intercourse with Men

10. Forsake not an old friend,
    For a new one is not like him (?).
    New wine is a new friend,
    And when it is old, then thou drinkest it.
11. Envy not a godless man,
    For thou knowest not what his day [will bring
       forth].
12. Take no pleasure in the proud man who pros-
       pereth,
    Remember that until death he shall not go
       unpunished.
13. Be far from the man that hath power to kill,
    And fear not then] the terrors of death;
    And if thou drawest nigh to him commit no fault,
    Lest he take away thy life.
    Know that thou walkest in the midst of snares,
    And treadest among nets.
14. As far as thou art able take counsel with thy
       neighbour,
    And converse with the wise.
15. Let thy communing be with a man of under-
       standing,
    And all thy converse in the Law of the Lord.
16. Let upright men be partakers at thy table,
    And let the fear of God be thy boast.

1 The text of *Heb.* is corrupt.

C

IX. 17–X. 18. **The Art of Ruling**

H. 17. By the cunning-handed a work of art is formed,
    So must a ruler over his people be wise in
    speech.

18. Terrible in the city is the loud-tongued man,
    And hated is he that is hasty in speech.

X. 1. A wise ruler instructeth his people,
    And the dominion of one that is discerning is
    well-ordered.

2. As the ruler of a people so are his officers,
    And as the head of a city so are the inhabitants
    thereof.

3. A reckless king is the ruin of the city,
    And a city becometh populous through the
    insight of its princes.

5. In the hand of God is the dominion of every
    man,
    And in the sight of a ruler doth He set His
    majesty.[1]

4. In the hand of God is the dominion of the world,
    And He placeth over it the right man.[2]

6. Render not evil to a neighbour for any trans-
    gression,
    And walk not in the way of pride.

7. Hateful to the Lord and men is pride,
    And to both of them oppression is a crime.

8. Dominion goeth from one nation to another,
    Because of the violence of pride.

9. How should dust and ashes be proud,
    Whose entrails decay [even] in his life-time?

10. The ravage of disease mocketh the physician;
    A king to-day, to-morrow he falleth.

11. When man dieth he inheriteth worms,
    And maggot and lice and creeping things.

12. The beginning of pride is when a man becometh
    shameless,
    And his heart departeth from his Maker.

---

[1] Verses 4, 5 are in the wrong order in *Heb.*
[2] *I. e.* the man for his time.

13. The gathering-place of insolence is sin,   H.
    And its source bubbleth over with depravity.
    Therefore hath God punished him in wondrous
      fashion,
    And smitten him utterly.
14. The throne of the proud hath God overturned,
    And He hath set the humble in place thereof.
15. The roots of nations hath God plucked up,   G.
    And set up the humble in their place.[1]
16. The [very] traces of the proud hath God obliter- H.
    ated,
    And hath rooted them from the depths [2] of the
    earth.
17. He hath torn them up from the earth, and rooted
    them out,
    And hath wiped out their memory from among
    men.
18. For insolence is not fitting for men,
    Nor fierce wrath from those born of woman.

X. 19–25. **Honour to whom Honour is due**

19. An honourable race is what?   The race of men.
    What manner of seed is honourable?   They G.
    that fear the Lord.[3]
    What manner of seed is without honour?   The
    seed of man.[3]
    A contemptible seed is that which transgresseth H.
    the commandment.
20. Among brethren their head is honoured,
    And he that feareth God among His people.
[21. The fear of the Lord is the beginning of accept- G.
    ance [with Him],
    But obstinacy and pride are the beginning of
    casting away.]
22. Sojourner and stranger, foreigner and poor man, H.
    Their glory is the fear of God.
23. The poor man of insight is not to be despised,
    And the violent man is not to be honoured.

---

[1] Verse 15 is not extant in *Heb.*   [2] *Lit.* " foundations."
[3] These lines are not extant in *Heb.*

H. 24. Prince, governor, and ruler are had in respect,
    But none is greater than he who feareth God.
   25. A wise servant [even] nobles serve,
G.   And a man of knowledge will not grumble [at
        that].[1]

X. 26-29. Self-esteem

H. 26. Play not the wise man in doing thy work,
    And esteem not thyself in the time of thy need.
   27. Better is he that worketh and hath wealth in
        abundance,
    Than he that esteemeth himself and lacketh
        sustenance.
 . 28. My son, esteem thyself in humility,
    And give it discretion, [for] so it is fitting.
   29. He that condemneth himself who will justify?
    And who will esteem him that dishonoureth
        himself?

X. 30–XI. 1. Wisdom, not Wealth, bringeth Honour

   30. There is a poor man who is honoured for his
        wisdom,
    And there is one that is honoured for his
        wealth.
   31. He that is honoured [in his poverty], how much
        more in his wealth!
    And he that is despised in his wealth, how much
        more [in his poverty]!
XI. 1. The wisdom of the poor man lifteth up his
        head,
    And causeth him to sit among princes.

XI. 2–13. Appearances are often Fallacious

   2. Praise no man for his beauty,
    And abhor no man unlovely in his appearance.

---

[1] The text of *Heb.* is mutilated.

3. A thing of nought is the bee among flying **H.**
   creatures,
   Yet chief among products is her fruit.
4. Him that is clothed in mourning mock not,[1]
   Nor despise those whose days are sorrowful;
   For wondrous are the works of the Lord,
   And hidden from men are His acts.
5. Many oppressed have sat on a throne,
   And those never thought of have worn a
   crown.[2]
6. Many exalted have been brought very low, and
   have been altogether abased,
   Yea, those who were honoured have been
   delivered up.
7. Before thou hast examined reject not,
   Consider first, and then rebuke.
8. My son, answer nothing before thou hast heard,
   And in the midst of a discourse speak not.
9. In that which concerns thee not enter not,[3]
   And in the strife of the overbearing meddle
   not.
10. My son, wherefore dost thou multiply thy
    business?
    Yea, he that hasteneth to increase [riches]
    shall not go unpunished.
    My son, if thou runnest thou wilt not attain,
    And though thou seek thou wilt not find.
11. One toileth, and laboureth, and runneth,
    And is so much the more behind;
12. Another is broken down, wandering in misery,
    Poor in vigour, and abounding in misfortune;[4]
    But the eye of the Lord looketh upon him for
    good,
    And He shaketh him up out of the stinking
    dust;
13. He lifteth up his head, and exalteth him,
    And many marvel at him.

[1] The text of *Heb.* is mutilated.
[2] Emended text.   [3] *Lit.* "strive not."
[4] Emended text; *Heb.* is defective.

XI. 14-28. **All Things are in the Hand of God**

H. 14. Good and evil, life and death,
    Poverty and wealth, are from the Lord.
15. Wisdom and insight, and discerning of things,
    Are from the Lord.
    Sin and upright paths,
    Are from the Lord.[1]
16. Foolishness and darkness were created for
    sinners,
    And [as for] the wicked, evil is with them.[1]
17. The gift of the Lord abideth for the righteous
    lastingly,
    And His good pleasure prospereth continually.
18. One waxeth rich through self-denial,
    And mortgageth his reward.[2]
19. When he saith : " I have found rest,
    And now will I eat of my goods,"—
    He knoweth not what the day will bring forth,
    He leaveth [them] to another, and dieth.
20. My son, stick to thy task, and take pleasure
    therein,[3]
    And grow old in thy work.
21. Marvel not at the ways of the wicked,[3]
    Trust in the Lord and wait for His light;
    For it is a light thing in the eyes of the Lord,
    Suddenly, in a moment, to enrich the poor.
22. The blessing of the Lord is the portion of the
    righteous,
    And in due time his hope shall flourish.
23. Say not, " What profit [is it] that I have done my
    work,
    And what is now left for me [to do] ? " [4]
24. Say not, " I have sufficient,
    What harm will [henceforth] happen unto
    me ? "

---

[1] Verses 15, 16 are in all probability not part of the original
text.
[2] The text of *Heb.* is uncertain.
[3] Emended text; *Heb.* is much mutilated.
[4] Emended text; *Heb.* is somewhat mutilated.

25. The joy of to-day maketh misfortune to be **H.**
    forgotten,
    And the misfortune of to-day maketh joy to
    be forgotten,
26. For it is easy in the sight of the Lord in the day **G.**
    of death
    To requite a man according to his ways.[1]
27. An evil time maketh delights to be forgotten, **H.**
    And the last end of a man shall declare con-
    cerning him.
28. Before death call no man happy,
    For in his latter end a man is known.

XI. 29–34. **Evil Companionship**

29. Not every man should be brought into one's
    house,
    For how many are the strokes of the slanderer !
30. As a decoy-bird in a cage, so is the heart of the
    insolent,
    And as a spy that looketh out for an unde-
    fended point.[2]
31. The back-biter turneth good to evil,
    And against the best that is in thee he speaketh
    ill.[3]
32. From a spark [burning] coals increase,
    And a man of Belial waiteth for blood.
33. Shrink from an evil man, for he bringeth forth
    evil,
    Why bring a lasting blemish upon thyself?
    Cling not to a godless man lest he overturn thy
    way,
    And turn thee from thy covenants.
34. Let a stranger dwell with thee, and he will
    estrange thy ways,
    And will alienate thee from thy home.

[1] Verse 26 is not extant in *Heb.*
[2] *Lit.* " nakedness."
[3] *Lit.* " And against thy choice things doth he conspire."

XII. 1–7. **Indiscriminate Benevolence**

H. 1. If thou doest good, know to whom thou doest good,
> That there may be a good return for thy well-doing.
> From a corrupt neighbour let thy way be warned,
> For he will estrange thee from those who are dear to thee.[1]

2. Do good to the righteous, and thou shalt find thy recompense;
> If not from him, then from the Lord.

3. No good 'cometh] to him who succoureth a wicked man,
> Moreover, it is no good work that he hath wrought.

5b. Weapons of bread give him not,[2]

5c. Wherefore should he attack thee with them?

5d. Twofold evil wilt thou obtain

5e. For all the good thou accordest him.

6. For God also hateth the evil,
> And to the ungodly He rendereth vengeance.

7 (4). Give to the good, but withhold from the evil;

5a. Refresh the humble, but give not to the impudent.[2]

XII. 8–XIII. 1. **False Friends**

8. In prosperity a friend is not known,
> And in adversity an enemy is not hidden.

9. When a man is in prosperity even an enemy is friendly,
> But in his adversity even a friend withdraweth.

10. Never trust an enemy,
> For as brass doth his malice corrode.

11. And even when he hearkeneth to thee and walketh humbly,
> Take good heed to have a fear of him.

---

[1] These lines are clearly out of place, cp. xi. 34.
[2] The order of verses 4–7 in *Heb.* differs from that in *Grk.*

Be unto him as one that brighteneth a mirror,[1] H.
   and he will find no opportunity to harm thee,
And know the end of jealousy.[2]

12. Let him stand beside thee,
   Lest he thrust thee aside and stand in thy place;
Set him not at thy right hand,
   Lest he seek thy seat,
And too late thou perceive [the truth of] my
   words,
And sigh because [of ignoring] my teaching.

13. Who pitieth a charmer bitten [by a serpent],
   Or any that approacheth a savage beast?

14. So is he that is companion to a godless man,
   And polluteth himself with iniquities.
He will not cease until a fire be kindled in him;[3]

15. When he cometh with thee he doth not reveal
   himself,
   And if thou fall, he doth not fall to help thee;
So long as thou standest he doth not show himself
   [as he is],
   But if thou stumble he doth not restrain
   himself.

16. With his lips an enemy speaketh sweetly,[4]
   But in his heart he deviseth deep pitfalls.
And, moreover, an enemy will weep with his eyes,
   But when occasion serveth he will not be
   satiated with blood.

17. If misfortune befall thee he will be found there,
   And as one ready to help he will seize thy heel;

18. He shaketh his head, and waveth his hand,
   And with much whispering he changeth his
   countenance.

XIII. 1. Whoso toucheth pitch, his hand is defiled,
   And the companion of a scorner will learn his
   way.

---

[1] Emended text.
[2] The text of *Heb.* in this line is corrupt; read, on the basis of *Grk.*: " And thou wilt know how to be rid of rust."
[3] This line has become misplaced, see xxiii. 16 f.
[4] Emended text.

XIII. 2-20. **Like consorteth with Like**

H. 2. That which is too heavy for thee raise not up,
 And consort not with one richer than thou.
 What companionship hath the pot with the cauldron?
 When the one smiteth the other is broken!

3. The rich doeth wrong and boasteth thereof,
 And the poor is wronged and [yet] hath to beseech.

4. If useful to him he maketh a slave of thee,
 And if thou break down he spareth thee not.

5. If thou hast aught he will give thee good words,
 And will impoverish thee yet grieve not at it.

6. If he have need of thee he will flatter thee,[1]
 And will smile on thee and ingratiate himself.[2]

G. He will speak thee fair, and say, What needest thou?[1]

7. And will shame thee by his hospitality.[3]

H. As long as it profiteth him he will befool thee,
 Twice [or] thrice he will fleece thee.[4]
 Later, when he seeth thee he will pass thee by,
 And shake his head at thee.

8. Take heed that thou be not over-proud,
 And be not like those who lack intelligence.

9. If a noble draw near, keep away [from him],
 The more will he [then] desire thy presence.[5]

10. Do not thyself draw near, lest thou be put at a distance,
 Yet stand not [too] far off, lest thou be forgotten.[6]

11. Venture not to be [too] free with him,
 And trust not the abundance of his talking;
 For by his much speaking he is trying thee,
 And while smiling he is probing thee.

---

[1] Emended text.
[2] *Lit.* "cause thee to trust him."
[3] These lines are omitted in *Heb.*
[4] The text of *Heb.* is uncertain.
[5] *Lit.* "cause thee to approach."
[6] Emended text.

12. Cruelty doth the tyrant practise, and he spareth **H.**
    not;
    Against the life of many doth he plot.
13. Take heed and be wary,
    And consort not with rough men.
[14. When thou hearest these things awake from thy **G.**
    sleep.
    All thy life love the Lord, and call upon Him
    for thy salvation.]
15. All flesh loveth its kind,   **H.**
    And every man his like.
16. All flesh consorteth according to its kind,
    And with his kind doth man associate.
17. What companionship is there between a wolf
    and a lamb?
    Even so [it is] if the wicked associateth with
    the righteous.
18. What kind of peace can there be between a hyena
    and a dog?   .
    Or what peace between rich and poor?
19. Food for the lion are the wild asses of the
    wilderness,
    Even so the pasture of the rich are the poor.
20. The abomination of pride is humility,
    Even so the abomination of the rich are the poor.

XIII. 21–23. **Rich and Poor**

21. When a rich man is in difficulties [1] he is supported
    by a friend,
    But when a poor man is in difficulties [1] he is
    thrust away by a friend.
22. A rich man speaketh, and his supporters are many,
    And his unseemly words [are pronounced]
    beautiful.
    A poor man speaketh, and they hiss him; [2]
    Yea, though he speak wisdom, they will not
    suffer him. [3]

    [1] *Lit.* " is shaken."
    [2] *Lit.* " they raise [the cry] Yah, yah ! "
    [3] *Lit.* " There is no place for him."

H. 23. When the rich man speaketh all keep silence,
        And his wisdom they extol to the clouds;
    When the poor man speaketh they say:
        " Who is this? "
    And if he stumble they will help to overthrow
        him.

XIII. 24–XIV. 2. Proverbs

24. Good is wealth if it be without sin,
        And evil is poverty if it come from sin.[1]
25. The heart of a man changeth his countenance,
        Whether for good or for evil.
26. A merry face is the sign of a happy heart,
        But sad eyes are signs of worry.[2]

XIV. 1. Blessed is the man whose mouth doth not
        grieve him,
        And who doth not let sorrow enter his heart.[2]
    2. Blessed is the man whose soul doth not reproach
        him,
        And whose hope hath not ceased.

XIV. 3–19. The Uses of Wealth

3. To the faint-hearted wealth is unfitting,
        And why should the miser [3] have gold?
4. He that withholdeth from himself gathereth for
        another,
        And a stranger will enjoy his goods.
5. He that harmeth himself whom will he benefit?
        And he hath no enjoyment in his goods.
6. There is none worse than he who harmeth himself,
        And the recompense of his evil is of his own
        making.[4]

G. 7. And even if he doeth good he doeth it uninten·
        tionally,[5]
        And at the last he revealeth his wickedness.[6]

[1] *Lit.* " that is due to presumption."
[2] Reconstructed text; *Heb.* is corrupt.
[3] *Lit.* " a man of evil eye," = an envious man.
[1] *Lit.* " is with him."   [5] *Lit.* " in forgetfulness."
[6] Verses 7, 8 are not extant in *Heb.*

8. Evil is he that envieth with his eye,   G.
　　Turning away his face and despising men.[1]
9. To the eye of the covetous his portion is [too] H.
　　small,
　　　And he that taketh his neighbour's portion
　　　hurteth his own soul.[2]
10. The eye of the envious hasteth after food,
　　　And naught is on his table.
　　A good eye causeth food to increase,
　　　And a dry fountain sendeth forth water upon
　　　[his] table.
11. My son, if thou hast aught, do well unto thyself,
　　　And look after thyself to thy utmost power.
12. Remember that death tarrieth not,
　　　Nor hath the decree of Sheol been told thee.
13. Before thou diest do good to him that loveth
　　　[thee],
　　　And according as thou hast prospered, give to
　　　him.
14. Refrain not from the joy of the present,[3]
　　　And upon the portion of a brother trespass not,
　　　and lust not after an evil desire.[4]
15. Wilt thou not leave thy wealth to another,
　　　And thy labour to them that cast lots?
16. Give and take, and indulge thy soul,
　　　For in Sheol there is no seeking of luxury;
　　And everything that is fitting to do,[5]
　　　Do in the sight of God.[5]
17. All flesh withereth [6] like a garment,
　　　And the everlasting decree is: "Thou shalt
　　　surely die!"
18. As leaves growing on a luxuriant tree,
　　　One fadeth and another shooteth forth,

---

[1] Verses 7, 8 are not extant in *Heb.*

[2] Emended text.

[3] *Lit.* "Withdraw not [thyself] from the good things of a
day."

[4] *Grk.*, which is to be preferred, reads: "And let not the
portion of a good desire pass thee by." The text of *Heb.* is
corrupt.   [5] These lines are probably a gloss.

[6] *Lit.* "weareth out."

H. So are the generations of flesh and blood,[1]
    One dieth and another flourisheth.[1]
19. All [man's] works will of a surety decay,
    And the labour of his hands followeth after
    him.

XIV. 20–27. Blessed are they that seek Wisdom

20. Blessed is the man that looketh on Wisdom,
    And that giveth heed to understanding,
21. That setteth his heart upon her ways,
    And giveth heed unto her paths,
22. Going forth after her like a spy,
    He looketh stealthily upon her enterings in,
23. He peereth in at her window,
    And hearkeneth at her doors;
24. He encampeth round about her house,
    And fixeth his pegs into her wall;
25. He pitcheth his tent close beside her,
    And dwelleth in a goodly dwelling;
26. He buildeth his nest in her foliage,
    And lodgeth among her branches;
27. Seeking refuge from the heat in her shade,
    He dwelleth within her habitations.

XV. 1–10. Wisdom is a Glad Possession

1. For he that feareth the Lord doeth this,
   And he that taketh hold of the Law findeth
   her.
2. And she will meet him as a mother,
   And as a youthful wife will she receive him;
3. And she will feed him with the bread of understanding,
   And give him the waters of knowledge to drink.
4. And he that stayeth upon her will not fall,
   Nor shall he that trusteth in her be ashamed;
5. And she will exalt him above his neighbour,
   And will open his mouth in the midst of the
   assembly.

---

[1] These lines stand in the margin of *Heb.*

H.

6. Joy and gladness shall he find,
   And she shall cause him to inherit an everlasting name.
7. Liars shall not obtain her,
   And the arrogant shall not look upon her;
8. Far is she from mockers,
   And untruthful men do not think of her.
9. Praise is not fitting in the mouth of the wicked,
   For it hath not been apportioned to him by
   God.
10. In the mouth of the wise praise is uttered,
    And he that is mighty in her shall teach her
    [to others].

XV. 11–20. **Free-will**

11. Say not, "From God is my transgression,"
    For that which He hateth made He not.
12. Say not, "[It is] He that made me to stumble,"
    For there is no need of evil men.
13. Evil and abomination doth the Lord hate,
    And He will not let it come nigh them that
    fear Him.
14. God created man from the beginning,
    And delivered him into the hand of him that
    spoileth him,[1]
    And placed him in the hand of his *Yetzer*.[2]
15. If thou [so] desirest, thou canst keep the com-
    mandment,
    And [it is] wisdom to do His good pleasure,
    And if thou trust Him, of a truth thou shalt live.
16. Poured out before thee [are] fire and water,
    Stretch forth thine hand unto that which thou
    desirest.
17. Life and death [are placed] before man,
    That which he desireth shall be given him.
18. Sufficient is the wisdom of the Lord,
    [He is] mighty in power, and seeth all things.

---

[1] This line is a gloss added for doctrinal purposes.
[2] A technical term meaning here "the evil tendency" or
"nature."

H. 19. And the eyes of God behold His works,
        And He knoweth every deed of man.
   20. He commanded no man to sin, ., ᵥᵥ.
        ᴺᵒʳ ᵍ ᵥ He strength, to meⱼ, es;
        And He hath no mercy on him that committeth
        falsehood,[1]
        Nor on him that betrayeth a secret.[1]

XVI. 1–5.   The Curse of Sinful Children

1. Desire not the sight [2] of unprofitable sons,
   And delight not in corrupt children.
2. Yea, and if they are fruitful, exult not because
   of them
   If they have not the fear of the Lord.
3. Trust not thou in their life,
       Nor rely upon their end,
       For there will not be for them a happy end.[3]
   For better is one that doeth the will [of the Lord]
       than a thousand wicked sons].[4]
       And to die childless than to have many un-
       profitable children and a presumptuous
       posterity.[4]
4. From one that is childless, but who feareth the
       Lord, a city is peopled,
       But through a race of treacherous men it is
       desolated.
5. Many things like these mine eye hath seen,
       And mightier things than these mine ear hath
       heard.

XVI. 6–16.   Woe unto the Wicked

6. In the assembly of the wicked a fire is kindled,
   And in an apostate nation wrath doth burn.
7. He forgave not the princes of old,
   Who revolted of yore in their might;

[1] These lines are later additions.   [2] *Lit.* " beauty."
[3] This line is a later addition.
[4] These lines are overloaded, but they contain the kernel
of the original.

8. He spared not the place where Lot sojourned,   **H.**
   Who were arrogant in their pride;
9. He spare' not the nation accursed,
   Dispo.... .d because of their si...
10. Thus [did it happen] to the six hundred thousand
    footmen,
    Who were destroyed ' _ the pride of their heart.
11. Yea, and if there be one tha. __ .iff-necked,
    A marvel would it be if he were not punished.
    For mercy and wrath are with Him,
       He forgiveth and pardoneth, but upon the
       wicked doth He cause His wrath to alight.
12. As great as His mercy is, so is His chastisement;
    [Each] man doth He judge according to his
    works.
13. The sinner shall not escape with his spoil,
    And He will not suffer the desire of the righteous
    to fail for ever.
14. Every one that doeth righteousness shall receive
    his reward,
    Yea, every man shall find it before him, accord-
    ing to his works.
[15. The Lord hardened the heart of Pharaoh who
    knew Him not,
    Whose works were manifest under the heavens;
    His mercies are seen by all His creation,
    And His light and His darkness hath He
    apportioned unto the children of men.]

XVI. 17–23. A Foolish Thought

17. Say not, " I am hidden from God,
    'And in the height who will remember me?
    [I shall not be noticed among so illustrious a
       people,
    'And what am I among the mass of the spirits
       of all the children of men? "
18. Behold the heavens and the heavens of the
    heavens,
    And the deep and the earth; [1]

       [1] *Grk.* adds : " [and all that in them is]."

    D

H. 19. When He treadeth upon them they shake,[1]
    And when He visiteth them they tremble;[2]
    Yea, the bottoms of the mountains, and the
        foundations of the world,
    When He looketh upon them tremble greatly.
20. " In truth, unto me He will not have respect,
    And as for my ways, who will mark them?
21. If I sin no eye beholdeth it,
    Or if I deal untruly in all secrecy, who will
        know it?
22. My righteous dealing, who declareth it?
    And what hope 'is there]? For the decree is
        distant ! "
23. They that lack understanding think these things,
    And a man of folly thinketh thus.

XVI. 24–30. Wisdom as seen in Creation

24. Hearken unto me, and accept my wisdom,
    And set your heart upon my words.
25. I will pour out my spirit by weight,
    And by measure will I declare my knowledge.
26. When God created His works from the beginning,
G.   After they were formed He assigned them
       their] portions,
27. He set in order their work for ever,
    And their authority unto their generations.
  They hunger not, neither do they labour,[3]
    And they cease not from their works.
28. None troubleth his neighbour,
    They never disobey His word.
29. And after these things the Lord looked upon the
      earth,
    And filled it with His good things.
30. He covered the face of the earth with every living
      thing;
    And unto it is their return.

[1] Emended text.
[2] *Grk.* adds: " [the whole world was made, and existeth, by His will]."
[3] Cod. א reads: " neither are they weak," which is to be preferred.

XVII. 1–14. **The Gifts of God**

1. The Lord created man from the earth,   **G.**
    And turned him thereunto again.
2. Days by number and a set time gave He them,
    And He gave them authority over the things
    upon her [*i. e.* the earth].
3. He clothed them with strength like unto Himself,
    And according to His own image made He them.
4. And He put the fear of them upon all flesh,
    And caused them to have power over beasts
    and birds.
[5. They received of the Lord the use of five powers,
    But as a sixth He also accorded them the gift
    of understanding,
    And as a seventh the Word, the interpreter
    of His powers.]
7. He filled them with skilfulness of understanding [1]
    And He showed them good things and evil.
6. Counsel, and tongue, and eyes, and ears,[2]
    And heart gave He them to understand,
8b. To show them the majesty of His works,
8a.   He set His eye upon their hearts,[3]
9. That they might declare the wonders of His
    works,
10.   And praise His holy Name.[4]
11. He set before them knowledge,
    And the law of life gave He them for an
    .   heritage.
12. He made an everlasting covenant with them, ·
    And showed them His judgements.
13. Their eyes beheld His glorious majesty,
    And their ear heard His glorious voice.

[1] *Syr.* reads : " With insight and understanding filled He
their heart "; this is to be preferred.
[2] *Syr.* reads : " He created for them tongue, etc."; this is
to be preferred.
[3] *Syr.* and some *Grk.* MSS. read : " And that they might
glory in His wondrous acts "; this is to be preferred.   The
order of verses 6–8 as given above follows that of *Syr.*, which
is more logical than the order in *Grk.*
[4] In *Grk.* verses 9–10 are in the wrong order.

G. 14. And He said unto them, Beware of all unrighteousness;
And He commanded them, each concerning his
neighbour.

XVII. 15–24. Divine Reward

15. Their ways are ever before Him,
They are not hid from His eyes.
[16. From their youth up all men's ways were
towards evil,
Neither were they able to make their hearts
to be] of flesh instead of stone.]
17. For every nation He appointed a ruler,
But Israel is the Lord's portion,
[18. Whom He brought up as His firstborn, with
severity,
Yet loving them [and] imparting to them the
light of His love, He forsook them not.]
19. All their works are [1] as the sun before Him,
And His eyes are continually upon their
ways.
20. Their iniquities are not hid from Him,
And all their sins are before the Lord.
[21. But the Lord, being merciful and knowing [them
to be made in] His own image,
Spared them and forsook them not, nor cast
them off.]
22. The righteousness of men is to Him as a signet,
And the mercy of man He preserveth as the
apple of an eye [granting repentance to His
sons and daughters.]
23. Afterwards He will rise up and recompense them,
And retribution will He bring upon their own
head.
24. Howbeit to them that repent doth He grant a
return,
And comforteth them that lose hope.[2]

[1] *Syr.* adds, probably rightly, " clear."
[2] *Lit.* " patience."

XVII. 25–32. **An Exhortation**

25. Turn unto the Lord and forsake sins,   **G.**
    Supplicate before His face and lessen offence.
26. Turn unto the Most High, and turn away from
    iniquity;
    [For He Himself will lead [thee] out of darkness
    unto the light of salvation]
    And vehemently hate the abominable thing.
27. Who will praise the Most High in Hades [1]
    In the place of those who live and give Him
    praise?
28. Thanksgiving perisheth from the dead as from
    one that existeth not,
    [But] he that liveth and is in health praiseth
    the Lord.
29. How great is the mercy of the Lord,
    And [His] forgiveness to them that turn unto
    Him.
30. For all things cannot be in men,[2]
    For a son of man is not immortal.[2]
31. What is brighter than the sun? Yet this faileth;
    And how much more man who [hath] the
    inclination of flesh and blood ! [3]
32. He looketh upon the host of the height of heaven,
    And [on] all men [who] are earth and ashes.

XVIII. 1–14. **God and Man**

1. He that liveth for ever created all things together,
2. The Lord alone shall be justified.
    [Who guideth the world in the hollow of His
    hand,
    And all things are obedient to His will;

---

[1] *Syr.* reads: " For what pleasure hath God in all that
perish in Hades "; this is to be preferred.

[2] *Syr.* reads:

" For it is not like this in man,
    Nor is [God's] thought like the thoughts of the children
    of men "; this is to be preferred.

[3] Emended text.

G. 3. For He is the King of all things, and they are
in His power.
He separateth among them the holy things from
the common.]

4. To none hath He given power to declare His
works,
Yea, who can trace out His mighty deeds?

5. Who can declare the might of His majesty,
And who can recount His mercies?

6. No man can take [from them] nor add [to them],
Nor can any trace out the marvellous acts of
the Lord.

7. When a man hath finished, then doth he but
begin,
And when he ceaseth he is in perplexity.

8. What is man, and what profit is there in him?
What is the good of him, and what the evil?

9. The number of man's days
Is great [if it reach] an hundred years;
[And eternal is the sleep of such, it is common]
to all.]

10. As a drop of water from the sea, or [as] a grain
of sand,
So are [man's] few years in the eternal day.

11. Therefore is the Lord longsuffering toward them,
And poureth out His mercy upon them.

12. He seeth and knoweth that their end [1] is evil,
Therefore doth He increase His forgiveness.

13. The mercy of man is upon his neighbour,
But the mercy of the Lord is upon all flesh,
Reproving, and chastening, and teaching,
And bringing back as a shepherd his flock.

14. He hath mercy on them that accept chastening,
And that diligently seek after His judgements.

XVIII. 15–18. Almsgiving

15. My son, put no blemish on [thy] good deeds,
Nor in [giving] any gift [cause] grief through
words;

[1] *Lit.* " overthrow."

16. Doth not the dew make the burning heat to **G.**
    cease?
    So is a word better than a gift.[1]
17. Lo, is not a word above a good gift? [2]
    And both belong to a gracious man.
18. A fool upbraideth ungraciously,
    And the gift of envious man consumeth the
    eyes.

XVIII. 19–29. Foresight

19. Learn before speaking,
    Heal before sickness.[3]
20. Before judgement examine thyself,
    And in the hour of visitation thou wilt find
    forgiveness.
21. Before thou art sick [4] humble thyself,
    And in time of sin show repentance.
22. Let nothing hinder thee from paying thy vows
    in due time,
    And wait not till death to be justified.
23. Before thou vowest, prepare thy vows,   **H.**
    And be not as one that tempteth God.[5]
24. Think of the wrath in the latter days,   **G.**
    And of the time of vengeance, when He turneth
    away His face.
25. Remember the time of famine in the time of
    plenty,
    And poverty and want in the days of wealth.
26. From morn till even the time changeth,
    And all things haste on before the Lord.

[1] *Syr.* reads: "So a word changeth [the character of] a gift"; this is to be preferred.
[2] *Syr.* reads: "For there is a good word which is better than a gift"; this is to be preferred.
[3] *Syr.* in verse 19 reads:

"Before thou fight, seek thee a helper;
Before thou art sick, seek thee a physician";

this is to be preferred.
[4] *Syr.* reads: "Before thou fall"; this is to be preferred.
[5] Emended text.

G. 27. A wise man is discreet in all things,
        And in days of sinning keepeth himself from
            offence.
   28. Every wise man knoweth knowledge,
        And to him that findeth her will he give thanks.[1]
   29. They that are wise in words[2] also show that
            they are wise
        In that they pour forth wise proverbs.
        [Better is trust in a single Master,
            Than with a dead heart to cling to a dead one.[3]]

XVIII. 30–XIX. 3.   Self-Control[4]

   30. Go not after thy desires,
        And refrain thyself from thine appetites.
   31. If thou grant to thy soul the gratification of [her]
            desire,
        Thou wilt make thyself a cause of rejoicing to
            thine enemies.
H. 32. Delight not thyself in overmuch luxury,
        For double is the poverty thereof.
   33. Be not a squanderer and a drunkard,
        Else will there be nothing in thy purse.
G.   [For thou wilt become a snare unto thine own life,
        And be much talked about.]
H. XIX. 1. He that doeth his [own] will not become rich,
        And he that despiseth small things will become
            wholly poor.
   2. Wine and women make the heart lustful,
G.   And he that cleaveth to harlots will become
            more reckless.[5]
   3. Moulder and worms will take possession of him,[5]
H.   And a brazen soul will destroy its owner.

---

[1] *Syr.* in verse 28 reads:

   " Every wise man teacheth wisdom,
        And they who know her must give thanks ";

this is to be preferred.
   [2] *Syr.* reads: " in teaching "; this is to be preferred.
   [3] *I. e.* an idol.
   [4] *Grk.* has the title: " Control of the soul."
   [5] These lines are not extant in *Heb.*

XIX. 4–12. **Garrulousness**

4. He that is hasty in reposing confidence is unwise,[1] G.
   And he that erreth sinneth against his own soul.
5. He that hath pleasure in his heart[2] shall be
   condemned,
   [But he that averteth his eye from pleasures
   crowneth his life.]
6. [He that controlleth his tongue liveth without
   strife.]
   But he that hateth talk hath the less malice.
7. Never repeat what is said,[3]
   And thou wilt derive no disadvantage;[4]
8. Speak not of it to friend or foe;
   And, unless it be a sin to thee, reveal it not,
9. For he hath heard thee and observed thee,
   And in [due] time he will hate thee.[5]
10. Hast thou heard anything? Let it die with thee;
    Be of good courage it will not burst thee.
11. A fool travaileth because of[6] a word,
    Even as a woman travaileth because of[6] a
    child.
12. [As] an arrow stuck in the fleshy thigh,
    So is a word in the belly of a fool.

XIX. 13–17. **Friendship**

13. Reprove a friend, it may be he did it not,[7]
    And if he have done anything, that he do it
    not again.

[1] *Lit.* " empty of heart."
[2] *Syr.* and some *Grk.* MSS. read : " in wickedness "; this is to be preferred.
[3] *Lit.* " a word."
[4] *Syr.* reads : " Then no one will reproach thee "; this is to be preferred.
[5] *Syr.* reads for verse 9 :

> " Lest he who hear thee hate thee,
>   And regard thee as an evil-doer ";

this is to be preferred.
[6] *Lit.* " In face of."
[7] *Syr.* reads : " Reprove a friend, that he do no evil ";
this is to be preferred.

G. 14. Reprove a friend, it may be he said it not,[1]
    And if he have said it, that he do it not again.
15. Reprove a friend, yet often there is slander,
    And believe not every word.
16. One man slippeth, though unintentionally,[2]
    And who hath not sinned [3] with his tongue!
17. Reprove thy neighbour, before thou threaten,
    And give place to the Law of the Most High.
[18. The fear of the Lord is the beginning of accept-
    ance ʃwith Him],
    And wisdom will gain love from Him.
19. The knowledge of the commandments of the Lord
    is life-giving instruction,
    And they who do the things that are pleasing
    unto Him shall pluck the fruit of the tree of
    immortality.]

XIX. 20–30. Wisdom and Craftiness

20. All wisdom is the fear of the Lord,
    And in all wisdom ⸢there is the fulfilling of
    the Law.
[21. And the knowledge of His omnipotence.
    A servant that saith unto his lord, " I will not
    do according to thy will," though he do so
    afterwards, angereth him that feedeth him.]
22. But the knowledge of wickedness is not wisdom,
    And the counsel of sinners is not understanding.
23. There is a wickedness [4] and the same is abomina-
    tion,
    And there is a fool who lacketh wisdom.[5]
24. Better is one that hath small understanding, and
    feareth,
    Than one that hath much prudence and trans-
    gresseth the Law.

---

[1] *Syr.* reads : " Reprove a friend, lest he speak [evil]."
[2] *Lit.* " not from the soul."
[3] *Syr.* and some *Grk.* cursives read " slipped."
[4] Two *Grk.* cursives read " prudence," which is to be preferred.
[5] *Syr.* reads " sins," which is to be preferred.

25. There is a subtle [form of] craftiness which is **G.**
 unrighteous,
    And there is one that dealeth tortuously to
    gain a judgement.
    [And there is a wise man who justifieth the
    judgement.]
26. There is one that doeth wickedly,[1] yet humbly
    and mournfully,
    But inwardly he is full of deceit.
27. [There is one] with downcast look, pretending to
    be deaf,
    But when unobserved [2] he will get the better
    of thee;
28. And if, for want of power, he be hindered from
    sinning,
    Will do evil when he findeth opportunity.
29. A man is known by his appearance,
    And a wise man, when thou meetest him,[3] is
    known by his face.
30. A man's attire, and the laughter of his teeth,
    And the gait [4] of a man proclaim the things
    concerning him.[5]

XX. 1–8. Silence and Speech

1. There is a reproof that is uncalled for,[6]
   And then] he that is silent is wise.
2. How good it is to reprove rather than to be wrath;[7]
   But let him that maketh confession be spared
   humiliation.[8]

[1] Two *Grk.* cursives read : " There is one that walketh ";
this is to be preferred.
 [2] *Lit.* " where he is not known."
 [3] *Syr.* rightly omits " when thou meetest him."
 [4] *Lit.* " the footsteps."
 [5] *Syr.* reads in verse 30 :
    " A man's attire proclaimeth his occupation,
        And his gait showeth what he is ";
this is to be preferred.
 [6] *Lit.* " not comely."
 [7] *Syr.* reads : " He that reproveth a sinner getteth no
thanks."
 [8] *Lit.* " be kept back from hurt."

G. [3. How good it is when he who is reproved mani-
        festeth repentance,
        For thus wilt thou escape wilful sin.]
H. 4. As is an eunuch that sojourneth with a virgin,
        So is he that would do right with violence.[1]
    5. One keepeth silence and is accounted wise,
        And another is despised for his much talking.
    6. One keepeth silence, having nought to say;
        And another keepeth silence, for he seeth [it is]
        a time ⌐for silence].
    7. The wise man is silent until the ⌐proper] time,
        But the arrogant and the scorner[2] take no
        note of the time.
G. 8. He that is abundant in word is abhorred,
        And he that taketh to himself authority is hated.

XX. 9-17.   Things are not always what they Seem

    9. ⌐Sometimes] it is advantageous[3] for a man to be
        in adversity,
        And there is a gain that turneth to loss.
   10. There is a gift that profiteth thee nothing,
        And there is a gift that bringeth a double
        recompense.
   11. ⌐Sometimes] there is humiliation through honour,
        And ⌐sometimes] a man from humiliation
        cometh to honour.[4]
   12. One buyeth much for little,
        Another payeth sevenfold.
H. 13. A wise man maketh himself beloved with few
        words,
        But the pleasantries of fools are wasted.[5]
G. 14. The gift of a fool profiteth thee not,
        [So it is with the niggardly man who only
        giveth under compulsion.]
        For his eyes are many instead of one.[6]

[1] In *Heb.* verse 4 is misplaced.
[2] Emended text.   [3] *Lit.* " there is prosperity."
[4] *Lit.* " lifteth up his head."   [5] Emended text.
[6] *I.e.* " For he looketh for a sevenfold recompense "
(= *Syr.*).

15. He giveth little and upbraideth much,   **G.**
      And openeth his mouth like a crier.
    To-day he lendeth and to-morrow he asketh it back,
      Hateful is such a one.[1]
16. The fool saith, " I have no friend,
      And my good deeds receive no thanks,
    They that eat my bread are evil-tongued."
      How oft—and how many they are—men laugh
      him to scorn.

XX. 18–20. Unseasonable Speech

18. A slip on the pavement is better than [a slip]
      of the tongue,
    Thus the fall of the wicked cometh swiftly.
19. A man without grace is [as] a tale out of season,
      It will be continually in the mouth of the
      ignorant.[2]
20. A parable from the mouth of a fool is rejected,
      For he uttereth it out of season.

XX. 21–23. Wilful, and Involuntary, Sin

21. One is hindered from sinning through lack [of
      opportunity],
      And when he resteth he is not troubled.
22. Another destroyeth his life through [sense of]
      shame,
      He loseth it through want of frankness.
23. And another, for shame's sake, promiseth to a
      friend,
      And maketh [3] him an enemy without reason.

XX. 24–26. The Liar

24. A foul blot in a man is a lie,
      It is [found] continually in the mouth of the
      ignorant.

---

[1] *Syr.* rightly adds : " to God and man."
[2] For verse 19 *Syr.* reads :
    " As the fat tail of a sheep, eaten without salt.
        So is a word spoken out of season ";
this is to be preferred.
[3] *Lit.* " obtaineth."

G. 25. Preferable is a thief to one who continually lieth,
But both shall inherit destruction.
26. The disposition of a liar is to be dishonourable.[1]

XX. 27–31. The Reward of the Wise [2]

27. The wise man advanceth himself in words,
And a prudent man pleaseth the great.
28. He that tilleth his land raiseth high his heap,
And he that pleaseth the great atoneth for
wrong.
29. Presents and gifts blind the eyes of the wise,
And as a muzzle on the mouth turn away
reproofs.
30. Hidden wisdom and concealed treasure,
What profit is there in either?
31. Better is a man that hideth his folly
Than a man that hideth his wisdom.
⌐32. Better is persistent endurance in seeking the Lord
Than a driver [3] of his own life without a master.]

XXI. 1–10. Sin and Sinners

1. My son, hast thou sinned?   Add not thereto;
And make supplication concerning thy former
sins.
2. Flee from sin as from the face of a serpent;
For if thou come near it, it will bite thee;
The teeth of a lion are the teeth thereof,
Slaying the souls of men.
3. Like a two-edged sword is all iniquity,
From the stroke thereof is no healing.
4. Tyranny and violence destroy wealth,
So the house of the arrogant is desolated.
5. Supplication from the mouth of a poor man
⌐reacheth]·unto His ears,
And his vindication cometh quickly.

[1] *Lit.* " dishonour."
[2] *Grk.* has the title, " Parabolic Sayings."
[3] *Lit.* " charioteer."

6. He that hateth reproof [walketh] in the path of a G.
   sinner,
   But he that feareth the Lord will turn [to Him]
   whole-heartedly.
7. He that is mighty in tongue is known afar
   off,
   But a man of understanding knoweth when he
   slippeth.[1]
8. He that buildeth his house with other men's
   money,
   Is as one gathering stones against winter.[2]
9. [Like] tow wrapped together is the gathering of
   the ungodly,
   And their end is a flame of fire.
10. The way of sinners is made smooth, without
    stones,
    And at the end thereof is the pit of Hades.

XXI. 11–17. The Godly and the Godless

11. He that observeth the Law becometh the master
    of the intent thereof,[3]
    And the fear of the Lord is the consummation
    of Wisdom.
12. He that is not wise [4] will not be instructed,
    And there is a wisdom [5] which maketh bitter-
    ness to abound.
13. The knowledge of a wise man aboundeth like a
    flood,[6]
    And his counsel is like a fountain of life.[7]

---

[1] *Syr.* in verse 7 reads—

   " The wise discerneth him that is before him,
      And spieth out the sinner at once ";

this is to be preferred.
  [2] *Syr.* and one *Grk.* cursive read : " for his sepulchral
mound "; this is to be preferred.
  [3] *Syr.* has rightly : " his natural tendency."
  [4] *Lit.* " crafty."
  [5] *Lit.* " craftiness."
  [6] *Syr.* better : " a spring of water."
  [7] *Syr.* better : " the water of life."

G. 14. The inward parts of a fool are like a broken
vessel,
He holdeth no knowledge.

15. If an understanding man hear a wise word,
He commendeth it, and addeth thereto;
The wanton man heareth, and it displeaseth
him,[1]
And he casteth it behind his back.

16. The discourse of a fool is like a burden on a
journey,
But upon the lips of the wise grace is found.

17. The utterance[2] of a prudent man is sought for in
the assembly,
And his words are pondered in the heart.

XXI. 18–28. The Godly Man and the Fool

18. As a house that is destroyed[3] so is wisdom to a
fool,
And the knowledge of an unwise man is [as]
talk without sense.[4]

19. ⌐As⌐ chains on ⌐their⌐ feet, ⌐so⌐ is instruction to
the foolish,
And as manacles on their right hand.

20. The fool lifteth up his voice with laughter,
But the wise[5] man scarcely smileth in silence.

21. As a golden ornament is instruction to the wise,
And as a bracelet upon their right arm.[6]

H. 22a. The foot of a fool hasteth into a house,
23b. But it is good manners[7] to stand outside.[7]
23a. The fool through the door looketh into a house,
22b. But the cautious man demeaneth himself
humbly.[8]

---

[1] *Syr.* reads : "If a foolish man hear it, he mocketh at
it"; this is to be preferred.
[2] *Lit.* "mouth."
[3] *Syr.* better "as a prison house."
[4] *Lit.* "unexamined words."
[5] *Lit.* "crafty."
[6] Verses 20, 21 have become misplaced.
[7] Emended text.
[8] In *Heb.* verses 22, 23 have become misplaced.

24. It is unseemly [1] for one to listen at the door, **G.**
  And the wise man is grieved at the disgrace
    [of it].
25. The lips of strangers [2] [only] repeat [3] what
    others say,[4]
  But the words of the wise are weighed in the
    balance.
26. The heart of fools is in their mouth,
  But the mouth of the wise is [in] their heart.
27. When the ungodly curseth his adversary [5]
  He curseth his own soul.
28. The whisperer defileth his own soul,
  And is hated wheresoever he sojourneth.

XXII. 1–2. Sloth

1. The slothful man is like a filthy stone,
  And every one hisseth at the shame thereof.[6]
2. A slothful man is like the filth of a dunghill,
  Every one that taketh it up shaketh it out of
    his hand.

XXII. 3–6. Evil Children

3. Shame [there is] to the father that begetteth an
    uninstructed [son],
  And a daughter is born to his loss.
4. A prudent daughter is an inheritance [7] to her
    husband,
  But she that bringeth shame is a grief to him
    that begat her.
5. She that is bold bringeth shame on her father
    and husband,
  And she is despised by both.

[1] *Lit.* " want of instruction."

[2] One *Grk.* cursive reads " babblers," probably rightly.

[3] Codd. BAC read: " are grieved at."

[4] *Lit.* " the things that are not theirs "; this is the reading
of one *Grk.* cursive, and is to be preferred.

[5] *Lit.* " Satan."

[6] *Syr.* reads : " Every one fleeth from the stench thereof ";
this is to be preferred.

[7] Emended text.

E

G. 6. [As] music in time of mourning, [so is] unseason-
       able talk ;
         But stripes and correction are at all times
         wisdom.[1]
    9. [Children who live comfortably in good circum-
       stances
         Conceal the origin of their parents,
   10. But children who grow up in arrogance and
       wantonness
         Besmirch the noble descent of their kin.][2]

XXII. 7-18.   The Fool

    7. He who teacheth a fool is [as] one that glueth
         together a potsherd,
         [Or as] one that awakeneth a sleeper out of a
         deep sleep.
    8. He that discourseth to a fool is as one discoursing
         to him that slumbereth,
         And at the end he saith, " What is it ? "
   11. Mourn for the dead, for his light hath failed,
         And mourn for a fool, for understanding hath
         failed him .
         Weep gently for the dead, for he hath found
         rest ;
         But the life of a fool is worse than death.
   12. The mourning for the dead is for seven days,
         But the mourning for a fool and an ungodly
         man [3] is for all the days of his life.
   13. Talk not much with a foolish man,
         And consort not with a man without under-
         standing,[4]
         [For being without sense he will altogether
         despise thee.]
         Beware of him lest thou have trouble,
         And thou become defiled when he shaketh
         himself ;   .

[1] Emended text.
[2] These verses, as their contents show, do not belong here.
[3] *Syr.* rightly omits: " and an ungodly man."
[4] *Syr.* rightly reads: " with [one that is] a pig."

Turn from him and thou wilt find rest,   **G.**
    And [so] thou wilt not be wearied with his
      folly.
14. What is heavier than lead,
    And what is its name but " Fool " ?
15. Sand and salt and a weight of iron
    Are easier to bear than a senseless man.
16. [As] timber girt and fixed into the wall
    Is not loosened by an earthquake,
    So a heart established on well-advised counsel
    Will not be fearful in time [of danger].
17. A heart fixed on thoughtful understanding
    Is as an ornament graven [1] on a polished
      wall.
18. Small stones [2] lying upon a high place
    Will not remain against the wind,
    So will the fearsome heart [full of] foolish
      imagination
    Be unable to withstand any terror.

XXII. 19–26. Friendship

19. A wound in the eye [3] maketh tears to flow,
    And a wound in the heart [3] severeth friendship. [3]
20. He that throweth stones at birds scareth them
      away,
    And he that reproacheth a friend dissolveth
      friendship.
21. Even if thou draw the sword against a friend,
    Despair not, for there is a way out.
22. If thou open thy mouth against a friend,
    Fear not, for there is a [way of] reconciliation ;
    But reproach and arrogance, and betrayal of a
      secret, and a deceitful blow,
    In [face of] these every friend will depart.
23. Acquire trust in [4] thy neighbour in poverty,
    That in his prosperity thou mayest rejoice ;

---

[1] Emended text.
[2] So Codd. AC and cursives; Bℵ read " poles."
[3] Emended text.
[4] *Syr.* reads : " Support," which is to be preferred.

G.   Remain steadfast to him in time of [his] affliction,
            That thou mayest be heir with him in his
              inheritance.
            [For not always is the [outward] appearance to
              be despised,
              Nor is the rich man devoid of understanding
                to be respected.]
24. Before the fire is vapour of the furnace and
        smoke,
      So revilings before bloodshed.[1]
25. I will not be ashamed to shelter a friend,
      And I will not hide myself from his face;[2]
26. And if evil happen unto him through thee,
      Whosoever heareth it will beware of thee.

XXII. 27–XXIII. 6.   **Self-Control**

27. O that one would set a watch over my mouth,
      And a seal of shrewdness upon my lips,
    That I fall not by means of them,
    And that my tongue destroy me not.

*[XXIII. 1–5 in Grk. have got out of order; the
text is also corrupt in parts; the following translation
is based partly on an emended Greek text and partly
on Syr.]*

XXIII. 2. O that one would set scourges over my
            mind,
          And the discipline of wisdom over my heart,
          That they spare me not for mine ignorances,
          And overlook not my sins;
3. That mine ignorances be not multiplied,
    And that my sins abound not,
    Lest I fall in the sight of mine adversaries,
    And mine enemy rejoice over me.

---

[1] Verse 24 seems to have got out of place.
[2] For verse 25 Syr. reads:

  " Be not ashamed of a friend who becometh poor,
    And hide not thyself from his face ";

this is to be preferred.

1*a* (= 4*a*). O Lord, Father, and Master of my life,   **G.**
1*b*. Abandon me not to their counsel.
4*b*. Give me not a proud look,[1]
    And turn away lust from me.
6. May the lust of the body [2] and chambering not
    overtake me,
    And give me not over to a shameless soul.

XXIII. 7–15.   Control of the Tongue [3]

7. Hear, my children, [concerning] the discipline of
    the mouth,
    He that keepeth [it] will not be ensnared;
8. But the sinner is ensnared by his lips,
    And the reviler and the arrogant will stumble
    through them.[4]
9. Accustom not thy mouth to an oath,
    And make not a habit of naming the Holy
    One.
10. For as a servant who is continually scourged
    Lacketh not 'the marks of] a blow,
    So he that sweareth and continually nameth [the
    Holy One
    Is not cleansed from sin.
11. A man of many oaths is filled with iniquity,
    And the scourge departeth not from his house;
    If he offend his sin will be upon him,
    And if he disregard it he sinneth doubly;
    And if he sweareth without need he shall not be
    justified,
    And his house will be filled with calamities.
12. There is a manner of speech that is to be com-
    pared with death,
    Let it not be found in the heritage of Jacob.

---

[1] *Lit.* " a lifting-up of the eyes."
[2] *Lit.* " appetites of the belly," *i. e.* greed.
[3] *Grk.* has the title, " Discipline of the Mouth."
[4] For this line *Syr.* reads : " And the fool stumbleth
through his mouth "; this is to be preferred.

G.   For from the godly all these things shall be put
      away [1]
   And they shall not wallow in sins.[1]
13. Accustom not thy mouth to unseemly manner
     of speech],
   For there is a sinful thing in that.
15. A man that is accustomed to disgraceful talk [2]
   Will not learn wisdom all his days.[3]
14. Remember thy father and thy mother
   When thou sittest in council among the mighty,
   Lest perchance thou stumble among them,
     And showest thyself a fool in thy manner [of
     speech],
   And dost wish thou hadst not been born,
   And cursest the day of thy birth.

XXIII. 16-27. Impurity

16. Two types of men multiply sins,
   And a third bringeth wrath :
   A lustful soul burning like fire,
     Which is not quenched till it be consumed ;
   A fornicator in the body of his flesh,

H.
   For he ceaseth not till the fire consume him ;
G. 17. And the fornicator to whom all bread is sweet,
   For he will not leave off till he die.
18. A man [there is] that goeth astray from his own
     bed,
   And saith in his heart : " Who seeth me ?
   Darkness is around me, and the walls hide me,
     And no man seeth me, of what shall I be afraid ?
   The Most High remembereth not my sins."
19. The eyes of men are his only] fear,
   And he perceiveth not that the eyes of the Lord

---

[1] For these two lines *Syr.* reads :

   " He that keepeth his soul from this shall live,
     And not wallow in sins " ;

this is to be preferred.
  [2] *Lit.* " words of reproach."
  [3] Verses 13 and 15 belong together.

Are ten thousand times brighter than the sun,   **G.**
  Beholding all the ways of men,
And looking into secret places.

20. For all things are known unto Him before they
  are created,
    So also [doth He see them] after they are
    perfected;

21. Such a man shall be punished in the streets of
  the city,
    And shall be taken where he suspecteth it
    not.

22. So also a wife that leaveth her husband,
  And bringeth in an heir by a stranger;

23. For, firstly, she is disobedient to the law of the
  Most High,
    And, secondly, she trespasseth against her own
    husband,
    And, thirdly, she committeth adultery through
    her fornication,
  And bringeth in children by a stranger.

24. She shall be led into the assembly,
  And upon her children there will be visitation.

25. Her children shall not spread out their roots,
  And her branches shall bear no fruit.

26. She will leave her memory for a curse,
  And her reproach shall not be blotted out.

27. And they that are left behind shall know
  That nothing is better than the fear of the
  Lord,
    And nothing sweeter than to observe
    The commandments of the Lord.

[28. To follow after God is great glory,
  And length of days it is for thee to be accepted
  of Him.]

XXIV. 1-34.   The Praise of Wisdom [1]

1. Wisdom is her own praise,
  And is honoured in the midst of her people.

---

[1] This title occurs in *Grk.*

G.

2. She openeth her mouth in the assembly of the
    Most High,
    And is honoured in the presence of His might.[1]
3. "I came forth from the mouth of the Most High,
    And as a mist I covered the earth.
4. In the high places did I fix my abode,
    And my throne was in the pillar of cloud.
5. Alone I compassed the circuit of heaven,
    And in the depth of the abyss I walked.
6. In the waves of the sea, and in all the earth,
    And in every people and nation I gained a
    possession.
7. With all these I sought a resting-place,
    And said, In whose inheritance shall I lodge?
8. Then the Creator of all things gave me com-
    mandment,
    And He that created me fixed my dwelling-
    place for me,
    And He said, In Jacob let thy dwelling-place be,
    And in Israel take up thine inheritance.
9. He created me from the beginning, before the
    world;
    And I shall never fail.
10. In the holy tabernacle I ministered before Him,
    Moreover, in Zion was I established.
11. Likewise in the beloved city He caused me to
    rest,
    And in Jerusalem was my authority.
12. And I took root among an honoured people,
    In the portion of the Lord, and of His in-
    heritance.
13. I was exalted like a cedar in Libanus,
    And like a cypress on the mountains of Hermon.
14. I was exalted like a palm-tree on the sea-shore,
    And as rose-plants in Jericho;
    And as a fair olive-tree in the plain;
    Yea, I was exalted as a plane-tree.[2]

---

[1] *Syr.* reads: "hosts"; this is to be preferred.
[2] *Syr. Lat.* and some *Grk.* cursives rightly add: "by the
waters."

15. As cinnamon and aspalathus have I given a **G.**
     scent of perfumes,
   And as choice myrrh I spread abroad a pleasant
     odour;
   As galbanum, and onyx, and stacte;
     [I was] as the smoke of incense in the Taber-
     nacle.
16. I, as a terebinth, spread forth my branches,
   And my branches were branches of glory and
     grace.
17. As a vine I put forth grace,
   And my flowers are the fruit of glory and
     wealth.
[18. I am the mother of beauteous love,
   And of fear, and of knowledge, and of holy
     hope;
   I, the ever-existing one, am given to all my
     children,
   To those who are called by Him.]
19. Come unto me, ye that desire me,
   And be ye filled with my produce.
20. For my memorial is sweeter than honey,
   And the possession of me than honey-comb.
21. They that eat me still hunger [for me],
   And they that drink me still thirst [for me].
22. He that obeyeth me shall not be ashamed,   .
   And they that serve me shall not commit
     sin.
23. All these things are the book of the covenant of
     God Most High,
   The Law which Moses commanded [as] an
     heritage for the assemblies of Jacob.
[24. Faint not, [but] be strong in the Lord,
   And cleave unto Him that He may strengthen
     you.
   Cleave unto Him, the Lord, the Almighty;
   He is the one and only God, and beside Him
     there is no Saviour.]
25. Which filleth [men] with wisdom, like Pison,
   And like Tigris in the days of new [fruits];

G. 26. Which overfloweth, like Euphrates, with under-
        standing,
        And as Jordan in the days of harvest;
   27. Which maketh instruction to shine forth as the
        light,[1]
        And as Gihon in the days of vintage.
   28. The first man' knew her not perfectly,
        So also the last will not trace her out;
   29. For her understanding is more full than the sea,[2]
        And her counsel is greater than the deep." [2]
   30. And as for me, I was as a stream from the river,
        And I came forth as a conduit into a garden;
   31. I said, " I will water my garden,
        I will abundantly water my garden beds ";
        And lo, my stream became a river,
        And my river became a sea.
   32. Yet again will I bring instruction to light as the
        morning,
        And will make these things shine forth afar off.
   33. Yet again will I pour forth doctrine as prophecy,
        And leave it for eternal generations.
   34. Look ye and see', that I have not laboured for
        myself only,
        But for all those who diligently seek her.

XXV. 1-11. Things Beautiful and Things Hateful

   1. In three things was I beautiful,[3]
        And they are lovely in the sight of the Lord
        and of men :
        The concord of brethren, and the friendship of
        neighbours,
        And a wife and a husband suited to each other.
   2. Three types [of men] doth my soul hate,
        And I am greatly offended at their life,

[1] *Syr.* reads : " Which poureth forth, as the Nile, instruction "; this is to be preferred.
[2] Emended text.
[3] The text of *Grk.* is corrupt; *Syr.* reads : " Three things
hath my soul desired "; this is to be preferred.

The poor man that is arrogant and the rich man **H.**
    that is deceitful,
    And an old man that is an adulterer.
3. [If] in thy youth thou hast not gathered,
    How wilt thou find in thine old age?
4. How beautiful to grey hairs is judgement,   **G.**
    And for elders to know counsel.
5. How beautiful is the wisdom of old men,
    And thought and counsel to those who are
    honoured.
6. The crown of the aged is their much experience,
    And their glorying is the fear of the Lord.
7. Nine conceptions I accounted blessed in my heart,[1]
    And a tenth will I speak of with my tongue :
    A man that hath joy of his children,
    Who liveth and seeth the fall of his enemies.
8. Blessed is the husband of an understanding wife, **H.**
    That doth not plough with ox and ass.
    Blessed is he that hath not slipped with his tongue,
    And he that hath not served an inferior.[2]
9. Blessed is the man that hath found prudence,   **G.**
    And discourseth unto ears that listen.
10. How great is he that findeth wisdom,
    But he is not above him that feareth the Lord.
11. The fear of the Lord surpasseth everything,
    He that holdeth it, to whom shall he be likened?
[12. The beginning of the fear of the Lord is to love
    Him,
    And the beginning of faith is to cleave unto
    Him.]

XXV. 13–26.   An Evil Wife

13. Any wound, only not a heart-wound !   **H.**
    Any wickedness, only not the wickedness of a
    woman !

---

[1] *Syr.* reads : " Nine [types of men] have I conceived of,
[these] I accounted blessed "; this is to be preferred.
[2] Verse 8 is much mutilated, and its clauses are out of
order in *Heb.*; the translation given above is based on an
emended text.

G. 14. Any calamity, only not the calamity of haters !
         Any vengeance, only not the vengeance of
           enemies !
   15. There is no poison above the poison of a serpent,[1]
         And there is no wrath above the wrath of a
           woman.[1]
   16. I would rather dwell with a lion and a dragon,
         Than keep house with a wicked woman.
H. 17. The wickedness of a woman maketh black her
           look,
         And darkeneth her countenance like a bear's.
   18. In the midst of his friends her husband sitteth,
         And involuntarily [1] he sigheth bitterly.
   19. There is little malice like the malice of a woman,
         May the lot of the wicked fall upon her.
   20. As a sandy ascent to the feet of the aged,
         So is a woman of tongue to a quiet man.[2]
   21. Fall not through the beauty of a woman,
         And be not ensnared [3] by what she possesseth ;
   22. For hard slavery [3] and a disgrace it is,
         If a wife support her husband.
G. 23. A humbled heart and a sad countenance [4]
         And a heart-wound, is an evil wife.[4]
H.   Hands that hang down, and palsied knees
         For a wife that maketh not her husband happy.
   24. From a woman did sin originate,
         And because of her we all must die.
G. 25. Give not water an outlet,[4]
         Nor power to a wicked woman.[4]
   26. If she go not as thou would have her [4]
         Cut her off from thy flesh.[4]

XXVI. 1–4. A Good Wife

H. 1. A good wife,—blessed is her husband,
         The number of his days is doubled.
    2. A worthy wife cherisheth her husband,
G.   And he fulfilleth the years of his life in peace.

---

[1] Emended text.
[2] Emended text; in verse 20 *Heb.* is much mutilated.
[3] Emended text.   [4] Not extant in *Heb.*

3. A good wife is a good portion;   G.
    She shall be given as a portion to them that
       fear the Lord.
4. [Whether] rich or poor, his heart is cheerful,
    And his face is merry at all times.

XXVI. 5–12. A Wicked Wife

5. Of three things is my heart afraid,
    And concerning a fourth I am in great fear : [1]
    Slander in the city, a concourse of the rabble,
       And a false accusation; worse than death are
          they all;
6. Grief of heart and sorrow is a wife jealous of
       another;
    The scourge of the tongue communicating to
       all.[2]
7. [Like] a yoke of oxen shaken to and fro is a
       wicked woman;[3]
    He that taketh hold of her is as one grasping
       a scorpion.
8. Great wrath a drunken woman [doth cause];
    She doth not cover her own shame.
9. The whoredom of a woman is in the lifting up of
       her eyes.
    And she is known by her eyelids.
10. Upon a headstrong daughter keep watch,
    Lest, finding liberty, she use it for herself.
11. Look well after a shameless eye,
    And marvel not if it trespass against thee;
12. As a thirsty traveller openeth his mouth,
    And drinketh of any water that is near,
    So she sitteth down at every post,
    And openeth her quiver to any arrow.

[1] Following Cod. A (= Syr.).
[2] Syr. reads: " The scourge of the tongue are they all,"
i. e. the things just mentioned; this is to be preferred.
[3] Syr. reads: " A hard yoke is a wicked woman "; this
is to be preferred.

XXVI. 13–18. A Good Wife

G. 13. The grace of a wife delighteth her husband,
And her understanding fatteneth his bones.

14. A silent woman is a gift from the Lord,
And a well-instructed soul is beyond worth.

15. Grace upon grace is a shamefast woman,
And there is no weight [of gold] worth a continent soul.

16. [As] the sun arising in the highest places of the Lord,
[So] also is the beauty of a good wife in the ordering of [her husband's] house.

17. [As] the lamp shining on the holy candlestick,
[So] also is the beauty of a face upon a stately figure.

18. [As] the golden pillars upon the silver base,
[So] also are beautiful feet upon firm heels.[1]

XXVI. 19–27. A Later Addition to the Preceding

[19. My son, keep thyself healthy in the flower of thine age.
And give not thy strength unto strangers.

20. Having found a portion of good soil out of all the land,
Sow it with thine own seed, trusting in the goodness of thine own good birth;

21. Thus will thine offspring flourish,
And, having confidence in their noble descent, will become great.

22. A hired woman is as spittle,
But a married woman is accounted a tower of death to them that use her.

23. A godless woman shall be given to the man who regardeth not the Law as his portion;
But a devout one shall be given to him that feareth the Lord.

[1] Emended text.

24. A shameless woman despiseth shamefastness;   G.
   But a shamefast daughter showeth modesty
   even before her husband.
25. A headstrong woman is regarded as a dog,
   But she that hath shame feareth the Lord.
26. A woman that honoureth her own husband
   appeareth wise unto all,
      But she that dishonoureth [her husband] is
      known to all as one that is godless in her
      pride.
   Happy is the husband of a good wife,
   For the number of his years is doubled.
27. A loud-voiced and tongueful woman is like a
   trumpet that putteth enemies to flight ;
      And the soul of such a man will pass his life
      in the turmoils of war.]

XXVI. 28. Three Things which cause Sorrow

28. For two things my heart is grieved,
   And for a third cometh wrath upon me :
   A man of war in want through poverty,
   And men of understanding if they are despised,
   And one that turneth from righteousness to sin ;
   The Lord will prepare a sword for him.

XXVI. 29-XXVII. 3. The Temptations of Trade

29. With difficulty doth the merchant keep himself
   from wrongdoing,
   And a huckster will not be acquitted of sin.
XXVII. 1. Many have sinned for the sake of gain,[1]
   And he that seeketh to multiply [gains] turneth
   away his eye.
 2. [As] a nail sticketh fast between the joinings of
   stones,
      [So] doth sin thrust itself in[2] between buying
      and selling.
 3. If a man hold not diligently to the fear of the
   Lord,
   His house will be swiftly overthrown.

[1] So Cod. ℵ.   [2] Emended text.

XXVII. 4–7. The Appraising of Man's Worth

G. 4. When a sieve is shaken the refuse remaineth,
      So [it is with] the filth of a man in his reasoning.
H. 5. The potter's vessel is proved in the furnace.[1]
      And the test of a man is by means of examining
      him.[1]
    6. According to the cultivation of a tree so is its
      yield,
      [So] the thought of a man according to his
      nature.[1]
    7. Praise no man before taking stock of him,[1]
      For by taking stock of man he is discerned.[2]

XXVII. 8–10. Reward and Retribution

    8. If thou follow after righteousness thou wilt attain,
      And put it on as a robe of glory.
    9. Birds dwell with their kind,
G.   And truth returneth unto them that practise it.
    10. The lion waiteth for its prey,
      So sins for them that work iniquity.

XXVII. 11–15. Varieties of Speech

    11. The discourse of the godly is always wisdom,
      But the fool changeth as the moon.
    12. In the midst of fools watch closely the time,
      But with a man that is thoughtful abide
      continually.
    13. The discourse of fools is an annoyance,
      And their laughter is sinful wantonness.
    14. The talk of a man of many oaths[3] maketh the
      hair stand on end,
      And their strife [demandeth] a stopping of
      the ears.
    15. A shedding of blood is the strife of the proud,
      And their reviling is grievous hearing.

[1] Emended text.
[2] *Lit.* " For this is the trial of men."
[3] *Syr.* reads : " The oath of the godless "; this is to be
preferred.

XXVII. 16–21. **The Betrayal of Secrets**

16. He who revealeth secrets destroyeth trust, G.
    And will find no friend to his mind.
17. Love a friend and keep faith with him,
    But if thou reveal his secrets follow not after
    him ;
18. For as a man that hath destroyed his enemy,
    So hast thou destroyed the friendship of thy
    neighbour.
19. And as a bird which thou hast loosed out of thy
    hand,
    So hast thou let thy neighbour go, and thou
    wilt not catch him again.
20. Pursue him not, for he is absent afar,
    And is escaped like a gazelle from a snare.
21. For a wound may be bound up, and for slander
    there is reconciliation,
    But he that revealeth secrets hath no hope.

XXVII. 22–24. **Insincerity**

22. He that winketh with his eye planneth evil
    things,
    And no man will remove him from it.[1]
23. Before thine eyes his mouth will speak sweetly,[2]
    And he will marvel at thy words ;
    But afterward he will alter his mouth,
    And with thy words will make a stumbling-
    block.
24. Many things I hate, but nothing like him,
    And the Lord will hate him too.

XXVII. 25–29. **Nemesis**

25. He that casteth a stone on high casteth it upon
    his own head,
    And a deceitful blow doth open wounds.[3]

[1] Two *Grk.* cursives read : " And he that knoweth him
keepeth far from him " ; this is to be preferred.
[2] So Codd. ℵAC (= *Lat*).
[3] *Lat.* reads : " And a deceitful blow apportions wounds
to the deceiver " ; this is to be preferred.

F

G. 26. He that diggeth a pit will fall into it,
>> And he that setteth a snare shall be taken therein.
27. He that doeth evil things,—they shall roll back upon him,
>> And he will not know whence they came unto him.
28. Mockery and reproach [come] from the proud,
>> And vengeance, like a lion, lieth in wait for them.
29. They that rejoice in the fall of the godly shall be taken in a snare,
>> And torment shall consume them before their death.

XXVII. 30–XXVIII. 7. Forgiveness

30. Wrath and anger, these also are abominations,
>> And a sinful man taketh possession of them.
XXVIII. 1. He that taketh vengeance shall find vengeance from the Lord,
>> And his sins He will, indeed. keep [in memory].
2. Forgive an injury [done thee] by thy neighbour,
>> And then, when thou prayest, thy sins will be forgiven.
3. One man cherisheth wrath against another,
>> And doth he seek healing from the Lord?
4. Upon a man like himself he hath no mercy,
>> And for his own sins doth he make supplication?
5. He being flesh nourisheth wrath,
>> Who will make atonement for his sins?
6. Remember thy last end and cease from enmity;
>> [Remember] corruption and death, and abide in the commandments.
7. Remember the commandments, and be not wrath with thy neighbour;
>> And [remember] the covenant of the Most High, and overlook ignorance.

XXVIII. 8–12. **Quarrelling**

8. Keep far from strife, and thou wilt diminish thy **G.**
    sins,[1]
    For a passionate man kindleth strife;
9. And a sinful man troubleth friends,
    And casteth calumny[2] in the midst of the
    peaceful.
10. According to its fuel so doth a fire burn,
    [3] And according to the vehemence of a strife
    so doth it increase;[4]
    And according to the strength of a man so is
    his wrath,
    And according to his wealth so doth he increase
    his wrath.
11. Strife begun in haste kindleth a fire,
    And a hasty quarrel leadeth to bloodshed.[5]
12. If thou blow upon a spark it kindleth, and if
    thou spit upon it, it is quenched;
    And both come forth from thy mouth.

XXVIII. 13–26. **The Evil Tongue**

13. Curse the whisperer and the double-tongued,
    For he hath destroyed many that were at peace.
14. The third tongue hath shaken many,
    And hath dispersed them from nation to
    nation;
    Even strong cities hath it destroyed,
    And overturned the houses of the great.
15. The third tongue hath cast out brave women,
    And deprived them of their labours;
16. He that giveth heed thereunto shall not find rest,
    Neither shall he dwell in quietude.

---

[1] *Syr.* reads: " and sins will keep far from thee "; this
is to be preferred.
[2] *Syr., Lat.,* rightly: " enmity."
[3] In Cod. B this line is erroneously placed at the end of
the verse.
[4] So rightly *Syr.* and two *Grk.* cursives, instead of " burn."
[5] *Lit.* " sheddeth blood."

G. 17. The stroke of a whip maketh a mark,
    But the stroke of a tongue breaketh bones.
18. Many have fallen by the edge of the sword,
    But not so many as have fallen by the tongue;
19. Happy is the man that is sheltered therefrom,
    That hath not passed through the wrath thereof,
    That hath not drawn the yoke thereof,
    And that hath not been bound with its bands.
20. For its yoke is a yoke of iron,
    And its bands are bands of brass;
21. The death thereof is an evil death,
    And Hades is more profitable than it.
22. [But] it hath no power over the godly,
    They shall not be burned in her flame;
23. They that forsake the Lord shall fall into it,
    And she shall burn them, and not be quenched;
    As a lion shall she be sent upon them,
    And as a leopard shall she destroy them.
24. Look that thou hedge thy possession about with thorns,
    And bind up thy silver and gold;
25. And make a balance and weight for thy words,
    And for thy mouth make a door and a bar.[1]
26. Take heed that thou slip not thereby,
    Lest thou fall before him that ensnareth.

XXIX. 1-13. **Lending and Borrowing**

1. He that lendeth to his neighbour showeth kindness,
    And he that strengthened him with his hand keepeth the commandments.
2. Lend to thy neighbour in time of his need,
    And repay thy neighbour at the appointed time.
3. Confirm thy word, and keep faith with him;
    And [so] shalt thou always have what thou needest.

[1] The order of the clauses in verses 24, 25 is more logical in *Syr.*, viz. 24*a*, 25*b*, 24*b*, 25*a*.

G.

4. Many have reckoned a loan as a windfall,
   And have brought trouble on them that helped
   them.
5. Until he receive it he kisseth thy hand,
   And speaketh humbly about his neighbour's
   money;
   But when payment is due he prolongeth the time,
   And returneth heavy words, and complaineth
   of [the shortness of] the time.[1]
6. And if he is able [to repay], with difficulty will
   he receive half,
   And counteth it as a windfall;
   And if not [able to repay], he hath deprived him
   of his money,
   And hath made him an enemy without cause.[2]
   With cursings and railings he repayeth him,
   And instead of honour he repayeth him with
   insult.
7. Many have turned away [from lending] because
   of wickedness,
   They feared to be defrauded for nought.
8. Howbeit with the lowly man be longsuffering,
   And let him not wait for alms.
9. Help the poor for the commandment's sake,
   And according to his need send him not away
   empty.[3]
10. Lose money for a brother or a friend's sake,
    And let it not rust under a stone and be
    lost.[4]
11. Lay up thy treasure according to the command-
    ments of the Most High,
    And it shall profit thee more than gold.
12. Store up alms in thy treasure-chambers,
    And it shall deliver thee from all affliction;

[1] *Syr.* reads: "And after much time he repayeth"; this
is to be preferred.
[2] So Cod. A (= *Syr. Lat.*).
[3] For this line *Syr.* reads: "And grieve not for the loss";
this is to be preferred.
[4] *Syr.* reads: "under a stone or a wall"; this is to be
preferred.

G. 13. Better than a mighty shield and a heavy spear
       Will this avail thee against an enemy.

XXIX. 14–20. **Suretyship**

14. A good man becometh surety for his neighbour,
    But he that hath lost his sense of shame faileth
    him.
15. The kindness of a surety forget not,
    For he hath given his life for thee.
16. A sinner destroyeth the estate of a surety,
17. And he that is of an ungrateful mind faileth him
    that delivered him.
18. Suretyship hath undone many that were pros-
    pering,
    And hath tossed them about as a wave of the
    sea.
    Wealthy men hath it driven from their homes,
    And they wandered among strange nations.
19. The sinner that falleth in his suretyship [trans-
    gressing the commandments of the Lord]
    And he that undertaketh contracts for work,[1]
    falleth into judgements.
20. Help thy neighbour according to thy power,
    And take heed to thyself that thou fall not.

XXIX. 21–28. **Contentment**

21. The chief requisites for life are water and bread,
    And a garment, and a house to cover nakedness.[2]
22. Better the life of a poor man under a shelter of
    logs,
    Than sumptuous fare among strangers.
23. Be contented with little or much.
24. An evil life [it is going] from house to house,
    For where one is a sojourner, one openeth not
    the mouth ;

---

[1] *Syr.* reads : " And followeth after sins " ; this is to be
preferred.
[2] *Lit.* " shame."

25. Thou entertainest and drinkest, and hast no **G.** thanks,[1]

　　Besides this thou wilt bear bitter things :

26. " Come hither, sojourner, furnish the table,

　　And if there is aught in thine hand, feed me " ;

27. [Or] : " Get out, sojourner, from the presence of honour,'

　　My brother is come as my guest, I need my house ! "

28. These things are grievous to a man that hath understanding :

　　Upbraiding ⌈concerning⌉ sojourning, and the reproach of a money-lender.

XXX. 1–13.　The Training of Children [2]

1. He that loveth his son will continue [to lay] stripes on him,

　　That he may have joy of him at the last.

2. He that chastiseth his son shall have profit of him,

　　And in the midst of his acquaintance shall he have glory of him.

3. He that teacheth his son will provoke his enemy to jealousy,

　　And before friends will he exult over him.

4. When his father dieth [it is] as though he died not,

　　For he hath left behind him one like him.

5. In his life he saw and rejoiced,

　　And in his death he was not grieved.

6. Against [his] enemies he hath left an avenger,

　　And to [his] friends one that requiteth favour.

7. He that pampereth [3] his son will bind up his wounds,

　　And his heart is troubled at every cry.

8. An unbroken horse becometh stubborn,

　　And a son left at large becometh headstrong.

---

[1] *Syr.* reads : " A stranger thou art [in that case], and drinkest contempt " ; this is to be preferred.

[2] Cod. B has the title, " Concerning Children."

[3] Emended text,

G. 9. Cocker thy child, and he will terrify thee;
  Play with him, and he will grieve thee.
 10. Laugh not with him lest he cause thee pain,
  And at the last thou gnash with thy teeth.
H. 11. Let him not have independence in his youth,
  And forgive not his mischievous acts.
 12. As a python pounceth upon a wild beast,
  So chastise his loins while he is yet young;
  Bow down his head in his youth,
  And beat his loins while he is yet small,
  Lest he become stubborn and rebel against thee,
  And there be born to thee vexation of spirit
  from him.
 13. Control thy son, and make his yoke heavy,
  Lest in his folly he lift himself up against thee.[1]

XXX. 14–20. **Health**

14. Better is a poor man healthy in body,
  Than a rich man stricken in his flesh.
15. I desire life in health rather than fine gold,
  And a cheerful spirit rather than pearls.
16. There is no wealth above the wealth of health.[2]
  And there is no good above ⸢that of⸣ a sound[3]
  heart.
17. Better is death than a life of vanity,
  And eternal rest than continual pain.
  Better is death than a wicked life,
  And descent to Sheol than continual pain.[4]
18. Good things poured out before a closed mouth
  Are like an offering placed before an idol;
19. What doth it profit the idols of the nations
  Which neither eat nor smell?
  So is he that hath wealth,
  But cannot enjoy it; [5]
20. He seeth it with his eyes, and groaneth,
  As an eunuch that embraceth a maiden.[5]

---

[1] So *Heb.* margin. [2] *Lit.* " a sound body."
[3] *Lit.* " good."
[4] Verse 17 occurs in this double form.
[5] The text of verses 19, 20 is mutilated.

XXX. 21–25. **Good Spirits**

21. Give not thyself to sorrow,   H.
     And be not worried with thine own counsel.
22. Heart-joy is life to a man,
     And happiness in a man putteth away anger.[1]
23. Beguile thy soul and cheer thy heart,
     And put vexation far from thee;
     For sorrow hath killed many,
     And there is no profit in vexation.
24. Envy and anger shorten days,
     And anxiety maketh grey before the time.

*[In Grk. a displacement takes place here; XXX. 25–
XXXIII. 16 come after XXXIII. 16–XXXVI. 11.
This displacement is found in all extant Grk. MSS.;
on the other hand, Heb., Syr. and Lat. preserve the
right order.]*

25 (= *Grk.* XXXIII. 13*b,c*). The sleep of him that is
     of a cheerful heart is like dainties,
     And his food agreeth with him.

XXXI. (XXXIV.) 1–4. **Poverty and Wealth**

1. Watching over wealth is·a weariness to the flesh,
    And the worry of it disturbeth sleep.
2. The worry of [getting] sustenance disturbeth
    slumber,
    And driveth away sleep more than severe
    sickness.
3. The rich man laboureth in gathering wealth,
    And if he rest it is to gather luxuries,
    Reproach driveth away a faithful friend,[2]
    But he who keepeth a secret loveth [his friend]
    as himself.[2]
    The poor man toileth to the lessening of his
    substance,[3]
    And if he rest he becometh needy.

[1] *Grk.* reads: " prolongeth days "; this is to be preferred.
[2] These lines, as their contents show, are not in their proper
place; cf. xxvii. 16, 17.   [3] *Lit.* " house."

H. 4. The poor man laboureth to the lessening of his
      strength,
      And if he rest it is no rest to him.[1]

XXXI. (XXXIV.) 5–11. Mammon

5. He that runneth after gold will not be guiltless,
    And he that loveth gain will go astray thereby.
6. Many there are who have been entangled through
      gold,
    And they that put their trust in pearls [have
      been ensnared].
    And they were not able [2] to deliver themselves
      from evil,[3]
    Nor yet to save themselves in the day of wrath.[3]
7. It is a stumbling-block for the foolish,
    And the simpleton is ensnared thereby.
8. Blessed is the man that is found perfect,
    That hath not gone astray after Mammon.
9. Who is he? that we may call him blessed,
    For he hath done a wonderful thing among
      his people.
10. Who hath been tested thereby, and hath remained
      unharmed?   .
    Let it be [accounted] to him for honour.
    Who might have fallen away, and did not fall
      away,
    And might have inflicted harm on his neigh-
      bour, but would not?
    For when the peace of his life increaseth
      I will be to thee for glory;
    Who hath blest and made his life perfect?
      I will be to thee for glory.[4]
11. Therefore shall his prosperity abide,
    And the assembly shall declare his praise.

---

[1] It is difficult to say which of these two couplets is the
original one, this or the preceding one.
[2] *Lit.* " they found not."
[3] *Grk.* rightly omits these lines.
[4] *Grk.* rightly omits the last four lines of verse 10.

XXXI. (XXXIV.) 12–24. **Instruction concerning Bread and Wine together** [1]

12. My son, if thou sittest at the table of some great H}
man,
Open not thy mouth [2] upon it.
Say not : " There is plenty here ! " [3]

13.   Remember that an envious [4] eye is an evil
thing ;
—God hateth an evil eye,
Nothing more evil hath He created ;
Therefore the eye weepeth for all things
And from the face tears flow(?).—[5]
God hath created nothing more evil than
the ʾevil] eye,
Therefore it weepeth because of all things ;

15. Honour thy neighbour as thyself,
And think over whatever may be distasteful
to thee.[6]

14. Stretch not out thine hand at that which he
looketh at,
And reach not thine hand with his into the dish ;

16. Eat like a man that which is set before thee,
And eat not greedily lest thou be despised.
Know that thy neighbour is ʾa man] like thee,[7]
And eat like a man that which is set before
thee,[7]
And be not greedy lest thou be despised.[7]

17. Leave off first for manners' sake,
And gobble not lest thou cause disgust.

18. And when thou sittest among many,
Stretch not out thine hand before thy neighbour.

19. Of a truth, a little sufficeth for a sensible man,
Then on his bed he needeth not to groan.

[1] This title occurs in *Heb*.   [2] *Lit*. "throat."
[3] *Lit*. " upon it."   [4] *Lit*. " evil."
[5] *Grk*. rightly omits the four lines in parenthesis.
[6] Verses 14 and 15, as their contents show, have got
misplaced.
[7] These lines are clearly a variant of verse 16 ; they are
rightly omitted in *Grk*.

H. 20. Pain and sleeplessness, distress and want of
         breath,
       And griping, are the lot of a foolish man;
       Healthy sleep [there is] for an unloaded stomach;
       He riseth in the morning refreshed.[1]
   21. But if thou art oppressed with [eating] dainties,
       Arise and vomit, so wilt thou have ease.
   22. Hearken, my son, and despise me not,
       And in the end thou shalt understand my words,
       - -Hearken, my son, and receive instruction,
       And mock not at me,
       And in the end thou wilt find my words.[2]—
       In all thy acts be moderate,
       And then no harm will touch thee.
   23. He who is seemly at table shall receive honour,[3]
       The testimony of his good behaviour standeth
         secure.
   24. He who misbehaveth at table will be talked of [4]
       ' in the gate,
       And the testimony of his evil standeth secure.

XXXI. (XXXIV). 25–31. **Wine**

   25. Moreover, when at wine, exercise restraint,[5]
       For wine [6] hath destroyed many.
   26. Like a furnace which trieth the work of the
         smith,
       So is wine in the quarrelling of scorners.
       —The discerning man proveth every work,
       So is strong drink in the contention of
         scorners.[7]- ·
   27. Water of life is wine to man,
       If he drink it in moderation.[8]

---

[1] *Lit.* " his soul is with him."   After verse 20 *Heb.* adds
six lines, but they are greatly mutilated.
    [2] The lines in parenthesis form a doublet; they are rightly
omitted in *Grk.*
    [3] *Lit.* " the lip shall bless."   [4] *Lit.* " murmured at."
    [5] *Lit.* " make thyself not valiant."   [6] *Lit.* " new wine."
    [7] The lines in parenthesis form a doublet; they are rightly
omitted in *Grk.*
    [8] *Lit.* " in its measure."

What life hath a man that lacketh new wine?   **H.**
  It was created from the beginning for gladness.[1]
28. Joy of heart, gladness and delight,
  Is wine drunk at the [right] time and in
    sufficiency.
29. Headache, derision, and shame,
  Is wine drunk in strife and anger.
30. Much wine is a snare to the fool,
  It diminisheth strength and increaseth wounds.
31. At a banquet of wine rebuke not a friend,
  And grieve him not in his merriment.[2]
  Speak not to him a reproachful word,[2]
  And quarrel not with him before others.[2]

XXXII. (XXXV.) 1–13. At the Banquet

1. Have they made thee ruler [of the feast] be not **G.**
    lifted up,[3]
  Be unto them as one of themselves;   **H.**
  Consider them [first], and then take thy seat;
2. Prepare for their wants [first], and then recline,
  That thou mayest rejoice in their glory,[4]
  And enjoy esteem for thy well-ordering.[5]
3. Speak, O elder, for this is thy part,
  Yet with discerning discretion, and hinder not
    the singing;
4. When the music beginneth[6] pour not forth talk,
  And display not thy wisdom when it is not
    wanted.[7]
5. As a signet of cornelian in a golden necklace,[8]
  So is good music at a banquet of wine.[9]
6. A setting of gold and an emerald signet
  Is the strain of music at pleasant wine-drinking.[9]

[1] Emended text (verse 27) based on two forms of the verse.
[2] Reconstructed text; these lines are much mutilated.
[3] The text of *Heb.* is almost entirely mutilated.
[4] *Grk.* " on their account "; this is to be preferred.
[5] *Lit.* " instruction."
[6] *Lit.* " In the place of music."
[7] The Hebrew idiom can only be rendered by a paraphrase,
it means " out of season," or the like.
[8] The meaning of the Hebrew is uncertain.
[9] There are unimportant variants to verses 5 and 6.

H. 7. Speak, young man, if thou art constrained [to
　　　do so],
　　　If asked twice or even thrice;
　8. Sum up thy speech, say much in little,
　　　Be as one who knoweth and can keep silent.
　9. Among elders assert not thyself,
　　　And among the noble be not perpetually talking.
　10. Before hail speedeth the lightning,
　　　And before the shamefast speedeth favour.
　11. At the time of departure be not the last,
　　　Depart home and be done with thy pleasure.
　　　<At the time of [rising from] table, multiply not
　　　words,>
　12. But if aught cometh into thine heart, speak,
　　　<Depart home and be done with thy pleasure,>
　　　In the fear of God, and not in senselessness.[1]
　13. For all these things bless thy Maker,
　　　Who satisfieth thee with His goodness.

XXXII. (XXXV.) 14–17. Contrast

　14. He that seeketh God receiveth discipline,
　　　And he that seeketh Him early obtaineth
　　　favour.[2]
　15. He that seeketh the Law shall gain her,
　　　But the hypocrite shall be ensnared thereby.
　16. He that feareth the Lord discerneth judgement,
　　　And causeth guiding lights to go forth from
　　　darkness;
　　　They that fear the Lord discern His judge-
　　　ment,
　　　And great wisdom shall they cause to go forth
　　　from their hearts.[3]
　17. The violent man shunneth reproofs,
　　　And wresteth the Law to suit his need.

[1] Verses 11 and 12 are confused through variants; the lines marked < > should be omitted.
[2] Verse 14 exists in several forms, but there is not a great difference between them.
[3] The two last lines of verse 16 are variants; with the last line cf. Job ix. 4 (Hebr.).

XXXII. (XXXV.) 18–24. **Forethought**

18. A man of counsel hideth not his understanding, **H.**
But the proud and scornful man will not
accept the Law.[1]
19. Do nothing without counsel,
That thou repent not after thine act.
20. Walk not in a path set with snares,
That thou stumble not twice at an obstacle.
21. Be not confident on a journey regarding plunder-
ing,
22. And in thy paths be wary.
23. In whatsoever thou doest take heed to thyself,
For he that doeth this keepeth the commandment.[2]
24. He that keepeth the Law guardeth himself,
And he that trusteth in the Lord shall not be
ashamed.

XXXIII. (XXXVI.) 1–3. **The Law**

1. No evil befalleth him that feareth the Lord,
But in temptation He will deliver him.[3] **G.**
2. He is not wise that hateth the Law, **H.**
And is tossed about like a ship in a storm.
3. A man of understanding discerneth the word,
And the Law is faithful as the inquiry of Urim.[3] **G.**

XXXIII. (XXXVI.) 4–6. **Thoughtlessness**

4. Prepare thy speech, and so let thyself be heard,
Bind up instruction, and [then] make answer.
5. [Like] a cart-wheel is the heart of a fool,
And as an axle-tree his [way of] thought.
6. A stallion horse is as a mocking friend,[4]
He neigheth under everyone that sitteth upon
him.

---

[1] Verse 18 exists in three slightly differing forms.
[2] There is an unimportant variant to verse 23.
[3] The text of *Heb*. is mutilated.
[4] *Syr*. reads: " Like a saddled horse is the love of a
fool "; this is to be preferred.

XXXIII. (XXXVI.) 7–15. **Divine Doings**

G.   7. Why doth one day excel another,[1]
When the light of every day in the year is
from the sun?

8. By the knowledge of the Lord were they distinguished,
And He varied seasons and feasts.

9. Some of them He exalted and hallowed,
And some of them He made ordinary days.

10. And all men are from the ground,
And Adam was created of earth.

11. In the abundance of His knowledge the Lord
distinguished them,
And made their ways various.

12. Some of them He blessed and exalted,
And some of them He sanctified and brought
nigh to Himself;
Some of them He cursed and humbled,
And overthrew them from their place.

13. As the clay of the potter in his hand,
All His ways are according to His good pleasure;
So men are in the hand of Him that made them,
To render unto them according to His judgement.

14. Over against evil ⌐standeth] good, and over against
death life;
Likewise over against the godly ⌐standeth] the
sinner.

15. Even thus look upon all the works of the Most High,
Two and two, one over against the other.

XXXIII. 16–18 (XXXVI. 16a, XXX. 25–27). **An Autobiographical Note**

16. And I, last of all, awoke,[2]
(XXX. 25). As one that gleaneth after the grape-
gatherers.
By the blessing of the Lord I made progress,
And, as a grape-gatherer, filled my winepress.

---

[1] *Syr.* reads: " Why is one day distinguished from another ? " This is to be preferred.
[2] *Syr.* reads: " came "; this is to be preferred.

(XXX. 26) 17. Consider that I laboured not for **G.**
myself alone,
But for all those who seek instruction.
(XXX. 27) 18. Hearken unto me, ye great ones of
the people,
And ye rulers of the congregation, give ear to me.

XXXIII. 19–23 (XXX. 28–32). **Independence**

(XXX. 28) 19. To son or wife, to brother or friend,
Give not power over thee while thou livest;
And give not thy goods to another,
Lest thou repent, and ask for them [again].
(XXX. 29) 20. While thou yet livest, and breath is
in thee,
Give not thyself to any.[1]
(XXX. 30) 21. For it is better that thy children ask
of thee,
Than that thou shouldest look to the hand of
thy sons.
(XXX. 31) 22. In all thy works keep the upper hand,
Let no stain come upon thine honour.
(XXX. 32) 23. In the day that thou endest thy life,
In the day of death, distribute thine inheritance.

XXXIII. 24–31 (XXX. 33–40). **Treatment of Subordinates**

(XXX. 33) 24. Fodder, and a stick, and burdens,
for an ass;
Bread, and discipline,[2] and work, for a servant.
(XXX. 34) 25. Set thy servant to work, and thou
wilt find rest,
Leave his hands idle, and he will seek liberty.
(XXX. 35) 26. Yoke and a thong will subdue the
neck,
And for an evil servant there are racks and
tortures.
(XXX. 36) 27. Put him to work that he be not idle;

---

[1] *Lit.* "Exchange not thyself for any [creature] of flesh."
[2] *I. e.* chastisement.

G. (XXX. 37) For idleness teacheth much mischief.
(XXX. 38) 28. Set him to [such] works as are suited
to him,
And if he obey not make his fetters heavy.
29. Be not excessive toward any creature,[1]
And do nothing without judgement.
(XXX. 39) 30. If thou hast a servant,[2] let him be as
thyself,
For with blood hast thou obtained him.
31. If thou hast a servant,[2] treat him as thyself,[3]
For as thine own soul thou hast need of him;
If thou maltreat him, and he depart and run
away,
On what way wilt thou seek him?

XXXIV. (XXXI.) 1–8. Dreams

1. Vain and false hopes are for a senseless man,[4]
And dreams elate[5] fools.
2. As one that catcheth at a shadow and pursueth
the wind,
So is he that setteth his mind on[6] dreams.
3. A vision of dreams is [as] this against that,[7]
The likeness of a face over against a face.
4. What can be made clean from an unclean thing?
And how can that which is true come from a
lie?
5. Divinations, and soothsayings, and dreams are
vain,
And as a woman in travail the heart conceiveth
fancies.[8]

[1] *Lit.* "flesh."
[2] *Syr.* reads : " If thou hast but one servant "; this is to
be preferred.
[3] Codd. ℵAC *Syr. Lat.* rightly read : " as thy brother."
[4] *Syr.* reads: " He who seeketh vanity findeth delusion ";
this is to be preferred.
[5] *Lit.* " give wings to."
[6] *Syr.* better " trusteth in."
[7] *Syr.* reads : " A dream is like a mirror "; this is to be
preferred.
[8] *Syr.* reads : " As thou hopest so doth thy heart see ";
this is to be preferred.

6. If they are not sent by the Most High in [time **G.** of] visitation,
   Give not thy heart unto them.
7. For dreams have led many astray,
   And they have fallen, trusting in them.
8. Without deceit shall the Law be fulfilled;
   And Wisdom in the mouth of one who is faithful is perfection.

XXXIV. (XXXI.) 9–20. **Wisdom is the Fear of the Lord**

9. A well-instructed man knoweth many things,
   And one of much experience expoundeth knowledge.
10. He that hath no experience knoweth ⌐but] few things,
11. But he who is well-versed [1] multiplieth his skill.
12. I have seen many things in my travels,
    And more than my words is my understanding; [2]
13. Oft-times was I in danger even unto death,
    But was saved thanks to these things.
14. The spirit of those who seek the Lord shall live,
15. For their hope is on Him Who saveth them,
16. He that feareth the Lord shall not be afraid,
    He shall not lose courage, for He is his hope.
17. Blessed is the soul of him that feareth the Lord;
18. On Whom doth he trust? And Who is his stay?
19. The eyes of the Lord are upon them that love Him,
    A mighty protection and a strong stay,
    A shelter from the scorching wind, a shelter from the mid-day sun,
    A guard from stumbling, a succour from falling;
20. One that refresheth the soul and lighteneth the eyes,
    That giveth healing, and life, and blessing.

---

[1] *Lit.* " who hath wandered."
[2] *Syr.* reads : " And many things have befallen me ";
this is to be preferred.

XXXIV. (XXXI.) 21–31. **Unacceptable Sacrifices**

G. 21. The sacrifice [1] of an unrighteous man is a mocking sacrifice,

22.   And the mockeries [2] of the wicked are not acceptable.

23. The Most High hath no pleasure in the offerings of the ungodly,

Neither is He pacified for sins by the multitude of sacrifices.

24. [As] one that slayeth a son in the sight of his father,

[So] is he that bringeth a sacrifice from the belongings of the poor.

25. The bread of the needy is the life of the poor,

He that depriveth him thereof is a man of blood.

26. He slayeth his neighbour that taketh away his means of living,

27. And a shedder of blood is he that depriveth the hireling of his hire.

28. One building, and another pulling down,

What profit have they but [useless] labour?

29. One praying, and another cursing,

To whose voice will the Master listen?

30. He who washeth after contact with] a dead body, and toucheth it again,

What profit hath he by his washing?

31. So a man fasting for his sins,

And going again and doing the same,

Who will hearken unto his prayer?

And what profit hath he in having humiliated himself?

XXXV. (XXXII.) 1–13. **Acceptable Sacrifices**

1. He that keepeth the Law multiplieth offerings,

2. And he that giveth heed to the commandments sacrificeth a peace-offering.

[1] Emended text.

[2] Reading uncertain; *Syr.* reads: " oblations "; this is to be preferred.

3. He that rendereth kindness offereth fine flour,   G.
4.   And he that giveth alms sacrificeth a thank-
        offering.
5. A pleasing thing unto the Lord it is to depart
        from wickedness,
        And a propitiation it is to turn away from
        unrighteousness.
6. Appear not in the presence of the Lord empty,
7.   For all these things [are due] because of the
        commandment.
8. The offering of a righteous man maketh the altar
        fat,
        And the sweet savour therefore [is] before the
        Most High.
9. The sacrifice of a righteous man is acceptable, ·
        And the memorial thereof shall not be forgotten.
10. With a good eye glorify the Lord,
        And stint not the firstfruits of thine hands.
11. In all thy works let thy countenance beam,   H.
        And with gladness sanctify thy tithe.
12. Give unto God according to His gift to thee,
        With a good eye and according as thy hand hath
        prospered ;
13. For a God of recompense is He,
        And sevenfold will He recompense thee.

XXXV. (XXXII.) 14-26. **The Helper of the Helpless**

14. Bribe [Him] not, for He will not accept [gifts],
15.   And trust not in a sacrifice of extortion ;
        For a God of justice is He,
        And with Him there is no partiality.
16. He will not show partiality to the detriment
        of [1] a poor man,
        But hearkeneth unto the supplications of the
        distressed.
17. He doth not ignore the cry of the orphan,
        Nor the widow when she poureth out her
        complaint.

[1] *Lit.* " against."

H. 18. Doth not the tear run down upon the cheek?
   19.   And [is there not] a sigh against him that
            causeth it to run down?
   20. [Such] a sigh is a bitterness accepted [of God],[1]
            And [such] a cry reacheth [2] to the clouds.
   21. The cry of the poor passeth through the clouds,
            And until it reacheth [God] resteth not;
        It will not cease [3] until God doth visit,
   22.   And the righteous Judge execute judgement.
        Yea, the Lord will not tarry,
            And the Mighty One will not refrain Himself,
        Till He smite the loins of the merciless,
   23.   And requite vengeance on the arrogant;
        Till He take away the sceptre of pride,
            And wholly destroy [4] the staff of wickedness;
   24. Till He render to a man [according to] his deed,
            And recompense him [according to] his thought;
   25. Till He plead the cause of His people,
            And make them glad with His salvation.
G. 26. Mercy is fitting in the time of their affliction,[5]
        As rain-clouds in the time of drought.[6]

XXXVI. 1–17 (XXXIII. 1–13a, XXXVI. 16b–22).
A Prayer

H.
   1. Save us, O God of all,
   2.   And cast Thy fear upon all the nations.
   3. Shake Thine hand against the strange people,
        That they may see Thy power.
   4. As Thou hast sanctified Thyself in us before their
        eyes,
        So sanctify Thyself in them before our eyes;
   5. That they may know, even as we know,
        That there is none other God but Thee.
   6. Renew the signs, and repeat the wonders,

---

[1] The text of *Heb*. is uncertain.   [2] *Lit.* " hasteneth."
[3] *Lit.* " remove."   [4] *Lit.* " cut down."
[5] This line is almost wholly mutilated in *Heb*.
[6] *Heb*. adds two lines, but only a few letters are decipherable.

7). Make glorious Thy hand and Thy right arm.   **H.**

7 (8). Awaken wrath, and pour out indignation,

(9).   Subdue the foe, and drive out the enemy.

8 (10). Hasten the end, and ordain the appointed time,

For who may say to Thee : " What art Thou doing ? "

9 (11). Let him that escapeth be devoured in raging **G.** fire,[1]

And may they that wrong Thy people find destruction.[2]

10 (12). Make an end of the head of the enemy's **H.** princes,

That saith, " There is none beside me ! "

11*a* (XXXIII. 13*a*). Gather all the tribes of Jacob,

11*b* (16*b*). That they may receive their inheritance, as in days of old.

12 (17). Have mercy upon the people that is called by Thy name,

Israel whom Thou didst surname Firstborn.

13 (18). Have mercy upon Thy holy city,

Jerusalem, the place of Thy dwelling.

14 (19). Fill Zion with Thy majesty,

And Thy Temple with Thy glory.

15 (20). Give testimony to the first of Thy works,

And establish the vision spoken in Thy name.

16 (21). Give the reward unto them that wait for Thee,

That Thy prophets may be shown to be faithful.

17 (22). Hear the prayer of Thy servants,

According to Thy favour towards Thy people.

That all the ends of the earth may know

That Thou art the Eternal God.

XXXVI. 18–20 (23–25). **Proverbs**

18 (23). Every meat doth the throat [3] eat,

Yet is one meat better than another.[4]   **G.**

---

[1] *Lit.* " in rage of fire."   [2] Verse 9 is omitted in *Heb.*
[3] *Heb.* margin " belly."   [4] This line is mutilated in *Heb.*

H. 19 (24). The palate tasteth the dainties that are
bestowed,[1]
And the discerning heart the dainties of falsehood.[2]

20 (25). A deceitful heart causeth sorrow,
But a man of experience turneth it back upon
him.[3]

XXXVI. 21–26 (26–31). Women

G. 21 (26). A woman will receive any man,
But one daughter is better than another
daughter.[4]

H. 22 (27). The beauty of a woman maketh bright the
countenance,
And excelleth every delight of the eye.

23 (28). And moreover, if there be in her a gentle [5]
tongue,
Her husband is not from among the sons of
men.[6]

24 (29). He that acquireth a wife hath the highest
possession,
A help meet for him, and a pillar of support.

25 (30). Without a hedge a vineyard is laid waste,
And without a wife [a man is] a wanderer and
homeless.

26 (31). Who trusteth an armed band
That rusheth from city to city?
So is the man that hath no rest,
Who resteth ⌜where he can⌝ when evening falls.

XXXVII. 1–6. Friendship

1. Every friend saith : " I have a friend,"
But there is a friend ⌜who is⌝ a friend in name
[only].

---

[1] So *Heb.* margin; the text is corrupt.
[2] The text of verse 19 is uncertain.
[3] *I. e.* upon him that causeth the sorrow; for " heart "
used in this personal sense see iii. 26.
[4] Verse 21 is almost wholly obliterated in *Heb.*
[5] *Lit.* " healing."   [6] *I. e.* he is as happy as the angels.

2. So there is a sorrow[1] that cometh nigh unto death, **H.**
   A soul-loved friend turned to an enemy.
3. O evil nature, wherefore wast thou created,[1]
   To fill the face of the world with deceit?
4. Evil is the friend that looketh to the table,
   But in time of stress standeth aloof.
5. A good friend [is he who] fighteth with the
   stranger,
   And taketh hold of the shield against the
   adversary.
6. Forget not a friend in [the time of] conflict,
   And forsake him not when thou takest the spoil.

XXXVII. 7–15. Counsellors

7. Every counsellor pointeth out the way,[2]
   But there is one that counselleth a way for
   his own advantage.
8. Of that counsellor let thy soul take heed,
   And know beforehand what is his interest;
   For he, too, will take thought for himself;
   Why should it fall out to his advantage?
9. And he will say to thee, How good is thy way!
   Then will he stand aloof and watch thine
   adversity.
10. Take not counsel with one who disliketh thee,[3]
    And hide thy secret from one that is jealous
    of thee.
11. (Take not counsel) with a woman concerning her
    rival,
    And an enemy [4] concerning his conflict,
    With a merchant concerning business,
    And with a buyer concerning selling,
    With an evil man concerning the showing of
    kindness,
    And with one who is merciless concerning
    man's happiness,[5]

---

[1] Emended text.
[2] *Lit.* " waveth the hand," cf. Isa. xiii. 2.
[3] Text uncertain.   [4] Emended text.
[5] *Lit.* " the welfare of flesh."

H.   With a worthless workman concerning his work,
      And with a yearly hireling concerning the
      sowing of seed,
G.   With an idle slave concerning much work,[1]—
      Trust not in these for any counsel![1]
H. 12. But rather with a man that feareth always,
      Whom thou knowest [to be] a keeper of the
      commandment,
      Whose heart is like thine heart,
      And if thou stumble he will be grieved for thee.
13. And also discern the counsel of [thine own]
      heart,
      For there is none more true to thee.
14. The heart of man declareth [to him] his oppor-
      tunities
      Better than seven watchmen on a watch-
      tower.
15. But in all these things entreat God,
      That He may direct thy steps in truth.

XXXVII. 16–26. Wisdom, True and False

16. The beginning of every action is speech,
      And before every act there is consideration.
17. The roots of the deliberations of the heart
      Throw out four branches :
18. Good and evil, life and death;
      But the tongue ruleth over them altogether.
19. There is a wise man who is wise to many,
      And to his own soul he showeth himself a fool;
20. And there is a wise man who is despised for his
      words,
      And is cut off from all pleasant food;
G. 21. For grace was not given him from the Lord,
      Because he is deprived of all wisdom.[2]
H. 22. And there is a wise man who is wise to his own
      soul,
      And the fruit of his knowledge is upon his
      body.

---

[1] These lines are wanting in *Heb.*
[2] Verse 21 is omitted in *Heb.*

23. And there is a wise man who is wise to his **H.**
     people,
     And the fruit of his knowledge is in their
     bodies.
25. The life of a man [numbers] few days,
     But the life of Israel [1] days without number.
24. He who is wise to his own soul shall be satisfied
     with enjoyment,
     And all who see him account him happy.
26. He who is wise [to his] people gaineth honour,
     And his name abideth to life eternal.

XXXVII. 27–31. **Discretion in Eating**

27. My son, in thy life prove thy soul,
     And see what is evil for it, and give it not that.
28. For not everything is good for everyone ;
     Every soul chooseth not of every kind.
29. Be not insatiable in every luxury,
     And give not thyself wholly [2] to every dainty.
30. For in much eating lurketh [3] sickness,
     And he that is surfeited draweth nigh unto
     loathing.
31. Through want of self-control [4] many have
     perished,
     But he that controlleth [5] himself prolongeth his
     life.

XXXVIII. 1–15. **The Physician**

1. Be friends with the physician since thou hast
    need of him.[6]
    For him also hath God ordained.
2. From God [it is] that the physician becometh wise,
    And from the king doth he receive gifts.
3. The skill of the physician lifteth up his head,
    So that he standeth in the presence of princes.
4. God hath created medicines out of the earth,

[1] Another reading is " Jeshurun."
[2] *Lit.* " be not poured out."   [3] *Lit.* " nesteth."
[4] *Lit.* " discipline."   [5] *Lit.* " guardeth."
[6] *Lit.* " according to his need."

H.   And let not a man of discernment despise
           them.

5. Was not water made sweet by the wood [1]
    In order to make known His power to all men?

6. And He gave to men discernment,
    To glory in His mighty works;

7. By them the physician relieveth pain,

8. Thus also the apothecary maketh his confection,
    That His work cease not,
    Nor health from the face of the earth.

9. My son, in sickness be not negligent;
    Pray unto God, for He can heal.

10. Turn from iniquity, and purify thy hands; [2]
    And from all transgressions cleanse thy heart.

G. 11. Give a meat-offering, and also a memorial, [3]

H.   And offer a fat sacrifice to the utmost of thy
           means.

G. 12. And also give a place to the physician; [4]

H.   And let ˹him˺ not be far from thee, for there
           is indeed need of him.

13. For there is a time when success is in his power; [5]

14. For he also maketh supplication to God
    To make his diagnosis successful,
    And the healing that it may give life.

15. He that sinneth against his Maker
    Behaveth proudly towards the physician.

XXXVIII. 16-23. Mourning

16. My son, let tears fall for the dead;
    Show thyself sorrowful, and mourn with a
    lamentation.
    Bury [6] his body according to his due,

---

[1] See Exod. xv. 23–25.

[2] Reconstructed text; *Heb.* is mutilated.

[3] This line is defective in *Heb.* with the exception of the last word.

[4] This line is for the most part defective in *Heb.*

[5] *Lit.* " hand."

[6] *Lit.* " gather," *i. e.* to his fathers.

And hide not thyself when he hath become a **H.**
corpse.

17. Make bitter thy weeping and passionate thy
wailing,
And make mourning such as befits him,
For a day or two to avoid scandal,[1]
And be comforted for thy sorrow.[2]

18. For out of sorrow cometh forth harm,
So sadness of heart bringeth down strength.

19. In calamity also sorrow abideth,   **G.**
And the life of a poor man is [hurtful] to the
heart.[3]   **H.**

20. Then turn not thy heart back again to him,[4]
Dismiss the remembrance of him, [yet] remember ⌈thy⌉ end.

21. Remember him not, for he hath no hope;
Thou canst not profit him, while thou harmest
thyself.

22. Remember his doom, for it is thy doom ⌈too⌉;
His yesterday, and thine to-day.

23. When the dead is at rest, let his memory rest;
And be consoled when his soul departeth.

XXXVIII. 24-30. The Craftsmen

24. The wisdom of the scribe increaseth wisdom,
And he that hath little business can become
wise.

25. How can he that holdeth the ox-goad become wise,
That glorieth in brandishing the lance? [5]
Who leadeth cattle, and turneth about oxen,
And whose discourse is with bullocks?

26. He setteth his heart on turning his furrows [6]   **G.**
And his anxiety is to have sufficient [7] fodder.   **H.**

---

[1] *Lit.* " on account of talking."
[2] Emended text.
[3] Verse 19 is omitted in *Heb.*
[4] *Heb.* margin reads : " Then let thy heart be no more
occupied with him"; this is to be preferred.
[5] The text of *Heb.* is corrupt.
[6] The text of *Heb.* is mutilated.
[7] *Lit.* " to complete."

H. 27. Likewise he that maketh carved work and cunning
            device,[1]

G.   Who passeth his time by night as by day; [2]
            They cut gravings of signets,
                And his diligence [3] is to make variety,
            He setteth his heart to make his likeness true,
                And his anxiety [4] is to finish his work.
    28. So the smith sitting by the anvil,
                And considering the unwrought iron;
            The vapour of the fire cracketh [5] his flesh,
                And in the heat of the furnace he striveth; [6]
            The sound of the hammer is continually in
                his ear,[7]
                And his eyes are upon the pattern of the
                vessel;
            He setteth his heart upon finishing his works,
                And his diligence [8] is to adorn [them] perfectly.
    29. So the potter sitting at his work,
                And turning about the wheel with his feet,
            Who is ever anxiously set at his work,
                And all his handiwork is by number;
    30. With his arm he fashioneth the clay,
                And he bendeth its strength before his feet;
            He applieth his heart to finish the glazing,
                And his diligence [8] is to clean the furnace.

XXXVIII. 31-34. **The Need of Craftsmen**

    31. All these rely upon their hands,
                And each is wise in his handiwork.
    32. Without them a city cannot be inhabited,
                And they sojourn not, neither do they walk
                up and down.[9]

---

    [1] The end of the line in *Heb.* is mutilated.
    [2] *Heb.* is wanting from here to xxxix. 15.
    [3] *Lit.* " patience."   [4] *Lit.* " wakefulness."
    [5] *Lit.* " melteth," so Codd. אA.
    [6] *Syr.* reads: " gloweth "; this is to be preferred.
    [7] *Lit.* " reneweth his ear," but this gives no sense.
    [8] *Lit.* " wakefulness."
    [9] *Grk.* gives no sense; *Syr.* reads: " Wherever they
sojourn [men] will not hunger "; this is to be preferred.

33. [But in the council of the people they are not G.
          sought for,]
       But in the assembly they will not be exalted,[1]
          And they will not [be able to] understand the
             covenant of judgement,[2]
       They shall not sit on the seat of the judge,[2]
          Neither shall they expound righteousness and
             judgement,
       And among parables they will not be found.[3]
34. But the fabric of the world will they maintain,[4]
       And their prayer [5] is in the handiwork of [their]
          craft.

XXXIX. 1–11. The Scribe

1. Not so he that giveth his soul,[6]
       And meditateth in the Law of the Most High;
    He searcheth out the wisdom of all the ancients,
       And is occupied in prophecies;
2. He preserveth the discourses of men of renown,
       And entereth into subtleties of parables;
3. He seeketh out the hidden things of proverbs,
       And is conversant with the dark things of
          parables.
4. He serveth among great men,
       And appeareth before a ruler,
    He travelleth in the land of alien nations,
       And hath tried both good and evil things
          among men.
5. He applieth his heart to resort early
       Unto the Lord that made him;
    But before the Most High doth he make
       supplication,
    And openeth his mouth in prayer,

---

[1] *Lit.* " mount on high."
[2] These lines are inverted in אA *Syr.*, rightly.
[3] *Syr.* reads: " Nor understand the proverbs of the
wise "; this is to be preferred.
[4] *Grk.* is corrupt; *Syr.* reads: " They understand the
work *they have wrought* " (the last words emended text).
[5] *Syr.*, rightly, " thought."
[6] *Syr.* rightly adds : " to the fear of the Lord."

G.   And maketh supplication for his sins.

6. If the Great Lord will,
    He shall be filled with the spirit of under-
      standing.
    He himself poureth forth words of wisdom,
    And giveth thanks to the Lord in prayer;
7. He himself directeth his counsel and knowledge,
    And in the secrets thereof doth he meditate.
8. He himself declareth the instruction of his
    teaching,[1]
    And glorieth in the Law of the covenant of
      the Lord.
9. Many praise his understanding,
    Never shall it [2] be blotted out,
    His memorial shall not cease,[3]
      And his name shall live unto generations of
      generations.

H. 10. His wisdom shall the Gentiles declare,
    And his praise shall the congregation tell
      forth.[4]

G. 11. If he continue he shall leave a name [greater
    than] a thousand;
    And if he die,[5] he shall add thereto.

XXXIX. 12–35. A Hymn of Praise

12. Yet more will I utter, which I have thought upon,
    For I am full as [the moon] at mid-month.
13. Hearken unto me, ye holy children, and bud
    forth
    As a rose growing by a brook [6] of water.
14. And as frankincense give forth a sweet odour,
    And put forth flowers as a lily;
    Spread forth a sweet smell, and sing a song of
      praise;
    Bless ye the Lord for all His works;

---

[1] *Syr.* better: " wise instruction."
[2] *Syr.* better: " his name."
[3] *Lit.* " depart."
[4] Verse 10 appears in *Heb.* in the margin against xliv. 15.
[5] *Lit.* " cease."   [6] So Codd. אAC.

15. O magnify His name,   G.
    And give utterance to His praise,
    With songs of the harp and of stringed instru- H.
        ments,
    And thus shall ye say, with a shout :
16. The works of God are all good,
    And for every need He provided in its time.
17 (21c). None may say : This is worse than that.
    (21d). For everything in its own time is excellent.[1]
    At His word the waters stood as a heap,[2]   G.
    And by the word[3] of His mouth His store- H.
        chamber.[4]
18. Forthwith (?) doth His good pleasure attain its
        end,
    And there is no restraint to His deliverance.[5]
19. The works of all flesh are before Him,
    And there is nothing hid from before His eyes ;
20. From everlasting to everlasting He beholdeth,
    Therefore there is no limit to His salvation,
    Nothing is small or insignificant with Him,
    And there is nothing too wonderful or too hard
        for Him.
21a. None may say : Wherefore is this?
21b.   For all hath been chosen according to its
        purpose.[6]
22. His blessing overfloweth as the Nile,
    And saturateth the world as the River.
23. Thus His indignation driveth out nations,
    And He turneth a watered land to salt.
24. The paths of the perfect are straight,
    [Even] so are they stumbling-blocks to the
        presumptuous.
25. Good things for the good hath He allotted from
        the beginning ;
    [Even] so to the evil ; good and evil.

[1] The two first lines of this verse are misplaced in *Heb.*
[2] This line is almost wholly mutilated in *Heb.*
[3] *Lit.* " that which goeth forth."
[4] The text of this line is probably corrupt.
[5] *Lit.* " salvation."
[6] See note to verse 17.

H

G. 26. The chief of all things necessary to the life of
man [1]

H.   Are water and fire, and iron and salt,

G.   And flour of wheat,[1] (*Heb.*) and milk and honey,

H.   The blood of the grape, oil and clothing.

27. All these are good to the good,
[Even] as for the evil they are turned to
evil.

G. 28. There are winds that are created for vengeance,
And in their wrath lay on their scourges
heavily ;
And in the time of the end they pour out their
strength,
And appease the wrath of Him that created
them.[2]

H. 29. Fire and hail, famine and pestilence,
These also are created for judgement.

30. Beasts of prey, scorpions and vipers,
And the avenging sword to slay the wicked,
All these are created for their uses,
And are in [His] treasure-house, and in [their]
time shall be requisitioned.[3]

31. When He commandeth them they rejoice,
And in their prescribed task they rebel not
against Him.[4]

32. Therefore from the beginning I stood firm,
And when I had considered it I set it down in
writing :

33. The works of God are all good,
They supply every need in its season.

34. None may say : This is worse than that,
For everything showeth its strength in its
season.

35. And now sing praises with all your heart,[5]
And bless the name of the Holy One.

---

[1] The text of *Heb.* is mutilated.
[2] The *Heb.* text of verse 27 is almost wholly obliterated.
[3] *Lit.* " visited."
[4] *Lit.* " His mouth."
[5] The margin of *Heb.* adds : " and mouth."

XL. 1–17. The Woes of Humanity

1. Much occupation hath God allotted,   H.
   And heavy is the yoke on the sons of men;
   From the day that he cometh forth from his
       mother's womb,
   Until the day of his returning to the mother
       of all living.

2. [As for] their thoughts, and fear of heart,   G.
   The idea of their expectation is the day of
       death.[1]

3. From him that sitteth upon a throne in exaltation, H.
   To him that sitteth [2] in dust and ashes;

4. From him that weareth a diadem and crown,
   To him that weareth a garment of hair,[3]

5. [There is but] anger and jealousy, anxiety and fear,
   Terror of death, strife and contention.
   And when he resteth upon his bed,
   The sleep of night doubleth his trouble.

6. For a short time, that he may rest for a moment,
       he is undisturbed,[4]
   And then by dreams is he disturbed.[5]
   He is troubled [6] by the vision of his soul,
   He is like a fugitive fleeing before the pursuer.

7. In the time of his deliverance [7] he is aroused,   G.
   And marvelleth that [there was] fear for
       nothing.[8]

8. With all flesh, both of man and beast,
   And upon sinners sevenfold more,[9]

9. [There is] pestilence and bloodshed, blight and H.
       drought,

[1] Verse 2 is wanting in *Heb.*; the text of *Grk.* is corrupt.
[2] *Heb.* margin : " is clothed."
[3] The text of *Heb.* is uncertain.
[4] Emended text, *Heb.* is corrupt.
[5] Reconstructed text; *Heb.* is mutilated, *Grk.* is corrupt, the line is wanting in *Syr.*
[6] So *Grk.*; *Heb.* is defective.
[7] *I. e.* in the time of sleep when he has respite from his troubles. .
[8] The text of *Grk.* is corrupt.
[9] Verses 7 and 8 are almost wholly mutilated in *Heb.*

H.   Devastation and destruction, famine and death.
   10. For the wicked evil was created,
        And because of him destruction departeth not.[1]
   11. All things that are from the earth return to the
        earth,
        And that which is from on high [returneth]
        on high.
G. 12. All bribery and injustice shall be blotted out,
        And faith shall abide for ever.[2]
   13. Wealth [gotten] by injustice is like a perennial
        torrent,
        And like a water-course mighty in a thunder-
        storm ;
   14. When it riseth rocks are rolled down,
        So doth it [3] suddenly come to an end for ever.
   15. A branch of violence [4] hath no shoot in it,
        And the root of the godless is upon a rocky
        crag ;
   16. It is like the sedge upon the bank of a river,
        Which is dried up before every other plant.[5]
H. 17. But kindness shall never be moved,
        And almsgiving endureth for ever.

XL. 18-27. The Fear of the Lord is the supreme Need

   18. A life of wine and strong drink is sweet,[6]
        But better than both is he that findeth a
        treasure.
   19. A child and a city establish a name,
        But better than both is he that findeth
        Wisdom.
        The offspring of cattle, and planting, make a
        name to flourish.
        But better than both is a loved woman.

---

[1] The negative has fallen out in *Heb*.
[2] Verse 12 is omitted in *Heb*.
[3] *I. e.* the wealth gotten by injustice.
[4] The reference is to one who acquires wealth unjustly.
[5] The *Heb*. text of verses 13-16 is uncertain.
[6] The text of *Heb*. is corrupt.

20. Wine and strong drink rejoice the heart,   H.
    But better than both is the affection of lovers.
21. Pipe and harp make sweet the song,
    But better than both is a pure tongue.
22. Grace and beauty charm thine eye,[1]   G.
    But better than both are the products of the H.
    field.
23. A friend and a companion meet opportunely,[2]   G.
    But better than both is a discreet wife.   H.
24. Brethren and succour [are a help] in time of G.
    affliction,[2]
    But better than both is righteousness [that] H.
    delivereth.
25. Gold and silver make the foot stand sure,[2]   G.
    But better than both is counsel esteemed.[2]
26. Wealth and strength lift up the heart,   H.
    But better than both is the fear of God.[3]
    In the fear of the Lord there is no want,
    And with it there is no need to seek [other]
    help.
27. The fear of God is as an Eden of blessing,
    And over all glory is its canopy.[4]

XL. 28–30. **The Beggar Life**

28. My son, lead not a beggar's life,[5]
    Better is one dead than one that beggeth.
29. A man that looketh upon a stranger's table,
    His life is not accounted life.
    A pollution of his soul are the dainties presented,

[1] The text of *Heb.* is mutilated.
[2] The text of *Heb.* in these lines is mutilated.
[3] One of the *Heb.* MSS. adds the following in the margin:

" All the days of the poor are evil,
    His roof is the lowest of roofs,
The rain of other roofs falls on his roof;
    Ben-Sira says, At night also.
And his vineyard is on the mountain-tops,
    And the soil of his vineyard falls on other vineyards."

[4] Quoted from Isa. iv. 5.
[5] *Lit.* " a life of gift lead not."

H.   And to a man of knowledge [they are] a cause
            of suffering.[1]
    30. In the mouth of a greedy man [2] begging is sweet,
        But within him it burneth like fire.

XLI. 1-4. **Death**

1. Ah, Death, how bitter is the remembrance of
    thee
    To him that liveth in peace in his habitation ;
    To him that is at ease, and prospereth in all,
    And that still hath strength to enjoy luxury.
2. Hail, Death, how welcome is thy decree
    To a luckless man, and that lacketh strength,
    That stumbleth and trippeth in everything,
    That is broken, and hath lost hope.
3. Fear not Death, [it is] thy destiny,
    Remember that the former and the latter share
    it with thee.
4. This is the portion of all flesh from God,
    And how canst thou reject the Law of the Most
    High?
    [Be it] for a thousand years, a hundred, or ten
    [that thou livest],—
    In Sheol there are no reproaches concerning life.

XLI. 5-13. **The Ungodly and the Righteous**

5. An abominable offspring is the generation of
    sinners,
    And a godless sprout is in the dwellings of the
    wicked.[3]
6. From the son of the unrighteous dominion shall
    be wrenched away,[4]
G.   And with their posterity shall be perpetual
            reproach.[5]

---

[1] *Lit.* " a suffering in the inward parts."
[2] *Lit.* " strong of soul."
[3] Emended text; *Heb.* is mutilated.
[4] The text of *Heb.* is uncertain.
[5] The text of *Heb.* is almost wholly mutilated. *Syr.*
reads : " And want shall ever abide with his seed "; this is
to be preferred.

7. A wicked father do the children curse,   **H.**
    For because of him do they suffer reproach.[1] **G.**
8. Woe unto you, ungodly men,[1]
    Who have forsaken the Law of the Most High
      God.[1]
9. If ye be fruitful [it will be] for harm,   **H.**
    And if ye bear children [it will be] for sighing;
    And if ye stumble [it will be] for everlasting joy,
    And if ye die [it will be] for a curse.
10. All that is of nought returneth to nought,
    So the godless man, from nothingness to
      nothingness.
11. Vanity is man concerning his body,
    But the name of the pious shall not be cut off.
12. Be in fear for thy name, for that abideth longer
      for thee
    Than thousands of treasures of wisdom.[2]
13. Life's goods [last] for limited days,[3]
    But the reward of a name for days without
      number.

XLI. 14–15. **Proverbs**

14. Hidden wisdom and concealed treasure,
    What is the use of either?
15. Better the man who hideth his folly,
    Than the man who hideth his wisdom.

XLI. 16–XLII. 8. **Instruction Concerning Shame** [4]

16 (14a). Hear, O children, instruction concerning
      shame,
    And be abashed according to my judgement.
   For not every kind of shame is meet to be
      retained,
    And not every kind of abashment is to be
      reproved.

[1] The text of *Heb.* is almost wholly mutilated.
[2] *Heb.* margin better : " precious treasures,"
[3] *Lit.* " days of number."
[4] This title is given in *Heb.*

H. 17. Be ashamed of a father and a mother of whore-
dom,
  Of a prince and ruler of lies,
18. Of a master and a mistress of deceit,
  Of an assembly and people of transgression,
  Of a comrade and friend of treachery,
19.   And of a place, where thou sojournest, of pride.[1]
  [Be ashamed] of altering an oath or a covenant,
  Of stretching out thine elbow at table,
  Of withholding a gift that is asked for,
21*a*.   Of turning away the face of thy friend,
G. 21*b*. Of taking away a portion or a gift,[2]
H. 20*a*.   Of being silent to one who greeteth,
20*b*. Of looking upon a woman that is a whore,
G. 21*c*.   Of gazing on a woman that hath a husband,[3]
22*a*. Of being busy with his maid,[3]
22*b*.   And of violating her bed,[3]
H. 22*c*. Of ¯speaking] to a friend with reproachful words,
22*d*.   And of upbraiding after thou hast given,
  XLII. 1. Of repeating a thing which thou hast
    heard,
  And of laying bare any secret counsel :
  So shalt thou be truly shamefast,
  And find favour in the sight of all living.
    [4] But of these things be not ashamed,
  And accept not persons unto sin :
2. Of the Law of the Most High, and the statute,
  And of justice, to render justice [even] to the
  wicked,
3. Of reckoning with a comrade and a [fellow-]
  traveller,
  And of dividing an inheritance or a property,
4. Of the small dust of the scales and balance,
  And of testing measure and weight,
  Of buying, as to whether [it be] little or much,

---

[1] So *Heb.* margin.
[2] The text of *Heb.* is mutilated.
[3] These lines are either wholly or in part mutilated in
Heb.
[4] In the English Versions, chap. xlii. begins here.

5.   And of profit from traffick with a merchant,[1] H.
      Of frequent correction of children,[2]   G.
      And of smiting an evil-disposed servant.[2]
6.   [3]For an evil wife a seal,[4]   H.
      And where many hands are a key.[5]
7.   Upon what is deposited make a mark,[5]
      And let giving and receiving all be in writing.
8.   Of the correction of the foolish and simple [be
         not ashamed],
         Or of [the correction of] the tottering grey-
            head occupied with whoredom :
      So shalt thou be truly well-advised,
      And a modest man before all living.

XLII. 9–14. The Care of Daughters

9.   A daughter is to a father a deceptive treasure,
         And the care of her putteth away sleep; [6]   G.
      In her youth lest she commit adultery,   H.
         And when she is married, lest she be hated; [6] G.
10.   In her virginity lest she be seduced,   H.
         And in the house of her husband, lest she be
            unfaithful,
         In the house of her father, lest she be with
            child,
         And in the house of her husband, lest she be
            barren.   .
11.   Keep a strict watch over a headstrong daughter,[6] G.
         Lest she make thee a laughing-stock [7] among
            thine enemies,
         A by-word in the city, and a running-together [8] H.
            of the people,

[1] The text of *Heb.* is uncertain.

[2] These lines are wanting in *Heb.*

[3] In verses 6 and 7 the construction changes, but they continue the enumeration of things of which one must not be ashamed.

[4] *I. e.* that the wife's property may be made secure to the husband.

[5] Emended text.

[6] The text in *Heb.* is mutilated. Verse 9 is quoted, in a slightly different form, in the Bab. Talmud, *Sanhedrin*, 100*b*.

[7] *Lit.* " a rejoicing."   [8] *Lit.* " an assembly."

H.   And shame be brought on thee in the gathering
         at the gate.
       In the place where she abideth let there be no
         lattice,
       And in the house where she sleepeth no entry
         round about.[1]
12. Let her not display her beauty before any man,[2]
       And in the house of women let her not gossip;
13. For from the garment cometh forth the moth,
       And from a woman a woman's wickedness.
14. Better the wickedness of a man than the goodness
         of a woman,
       And a daughter that causeth shame and poureth
         forth reproach.

XLII. 15–XLIII. 33. **God is the God of Nature**

15. Let me make mention of the works of God,
       And what I have seen will I also recount.
       By the word of God are His works,
        And He doeth His good pleasure according to
          His decree.
16. The rising sun is revealed over all,
       And the glory of the Lord upon all His works.
17. The holy ones [3] of God have not the power
        To recount the wondrous works of His might;
       [Yet] God hath given strength to His hosts
        To stand in the presence of His glory.
18. He searcheth out the deep, and the heart [of
         man],
       And discerneth all their secrets;
G.   For the Lord knoweth all knowledge,[4] .
       And He looketh into the signs of the world; [4]
H. 19. Declaring the things that are past and the things
         that shall be,
       And revealing the traces of hidden things.
20. No knowledge is lacking to Him,
       And not a thing escapeth Him.

---

[1] Emended text.   [2] *Lit.* " male."
[3] *I. e.* the angels.   [4] These lines are wanting in *Heb.*

21. The mighty works of His Wisdom hath He **G.**
    ordered; [1]
    One is He from everlasting;   **H.**
  Nothing hath been added, and nothing taken **G.**
    away [from them],[1]
    And He needeth none to instruct [Him].   **H.**
22. How desirable are all His works,   **G.**
    And as a spark are they to behold.[2]
23. All these things live and abide for ever,[3]
    And for every need all are obedient [to Him]. **H.**
24. All things are different, this from that,
    And He made not one of them superfluous.[4]
25. One thing surpasseth another in its goodness,
    And who shall be satiated in beholding [their]
        beauty?
XLIII. 1. The beauty of the height [of the heavens]
    is the pure firmament,
    And the vault of heaven is a spectacle of glory.[5]
  2. The sun when he goeth forth poureth out heat,[5]
    How terrible are the works of Jehovah!
  3. When it shineth at noon it scorcheth the world,
    Before its burning [heat] who can stand?
  4. A heated furnace maketh the metal to become
    heated,
    [But] the sending forth of the sun setteth
      mountains ablaze.
    The rays from the light [6] scorch the inhabited
      earth,
    And the light from the lamp [6] scorcheth the eyes.
  5. For great is Jehovah Who made it,
    And His word causeth His mighty one [6] to
      shine.[7]
  6. And also the moon He made for its due season,[8]
    To rule over periods for an everlasting sign.

[1] The text of *Heb.* is mutilated.
[2] Verse 22 is wanting in *Heb.*; in the second line of this
verse the *Grk.* text is corrupt.
[3] The text of *Heb.* is mutilated.   [4] Reconstructed text.
[5] Emended text.   [6] *I. e.* the sun.
[7] The text of *Heb.* is uncertain.
[8] Emended text; *Heb.* is uncertain.

H. 7. By her festivals and the appointed times [are
fixed],
G.   A light that waneth when she is come to the
full.[1]

8. Month by month she reneweth herself,
How wonderful[2] [is she] in her changing!
A beacon for the hosts on high,[1]
Paving the firmament with her shining.

9. The beauty of heaven, and its glory ⌐are⌐ the stars,
With their bright shining in the heights of
God.

10. At the word of God they stand as decreed,
And they sleep not in their watches.

11. Behold the rainbow, and bless the Maker thereof;
Exceeding majestic is it in its glory;

H. 12. It encompasseth the ⌐heavenly⌐ vault in its glory,
And the hand of God hath spread it out in
might.

13. His power sendeth out the lightning,
And maketh bright its flashes in judgement;

14. For it did He create a treasure-house,
G.   And clouds fly forth as fowls.[3]

15. By His mighty power He maketh strong the
clouds,[3]
And the hailstones are broken small.[3]

H. 17a. The voice of His thunder maketh the earth to
travail,

16a.   By His strength He shaketh the mountains.

16b. And the fear of Him stirreth up the south wind,

17b.   And the whirlwind of the north, and hurricane
and tempest.

17c. Like birds He sprinkleth His snow,

17d.   And like settling locusts is the coming down
thereof;

18. The beauty of its whiteness dazzleth the eyes,
And the heart is wonder-struck at the raining
down thereof.

---

[1] The text of *Heb.* is very uncertain.
[2] *Lit.* " terrible."
[3] The text of *Heb.* is mutilated.

19. Also the hoar-frost, He poureth it[1] out like salt,   **H.**
    And He causeth flowers to bloom like sapphires.[2]
20. The cold of the north-wind He causeth to blow,
    And hardeneth the pond like a bottle;[1]
    Upon every gathering of waters He spreadeth a crust,
    And the pond putteth on, as it were, a breast-plate.
21. The produce of the mountains He drieth up with scorching heat,
    And the springing grass of the meadows as [with] a flame.
22. Healing for all things is the dropping from the clouds,
    The dew which speedily refreshed the parched ground.
23. By His counsel hath He stilled the great deep,
    And hath planted islands in the midst of the deep.
24. They that go down to the sea declare its bounds,[3]
    And when our ears hear it we marvel.
25. Therein are marvels, the wonders of His works,
    All manner of living things, and monsters of the deep.
26. For His own sake He maketh His work to prosper,
    And by His word He worketh His pleasure.
27. Yet more things like these we will not add,
    And the end of the matter is : He is all.
28. We will still magnify, though we cannot fathom,
    For greater is He than all His works.
29. Exceeding terrible is Jehovah,
    And wonderful are His mighty works.
30. Ye that magnify Jehovah, lift up your voice,
    As much as ye are able, for there is yet more !
    Ye that exalt Him, renew your strength,
    And be not wearied, though ye cannot fathom Him.

---

[1] So *Heb.* margin; the text is corrupt.
[2] The reference is to the sparkling hoar-frost on shrubs.
[3] *Lit.* " end."

G. 31. Who hath seen Him that he may declare Him?
>   And who shall magnify Him as He is? [1]
H. 32. Many things, greater than these, are hidden,[2]
>   A few only, of His works, have I seen.
G. 33. Everything hath Jehovah made,
>   And to the godly hath He given wisdom.[2]

XLIV. 1–L. 24. Praise of the Fathers of Old [3]

H. 1. Let me now sing the praises of men of piety,
>   Of our fathers in their generations.
>   2. Great glory did the Most High allot them,
>   And they were great from the days of old.
>   3. [Men] who wielded dominion over the earth in
>   their royalty,
>   And men of renown in their might;
>   Counsellors in their discernment,
>   And seers in their prophetic power.
>   4. Princes of nations in their statesmanship,
>   And leaders in their penetration;
>   Wise in speech in their scribal office,
>   And speakers of wise sayings in their tradition;
>   5. Devisers of psalms according to rule,
>   And authors of written proverbs;
>   6. Men of ability and supported with strength,
>   And living at ease in their dwelling-places.
>   7. All these were honoured in their generation,
>   And in their days had glory.
>   8. Some of them [there are who] have left a name
>   That men might tell their praise;
>   9. And some of them [there are] who have no
>   memorial,
>   And they ceased even as they ceased;
>   They were as though they had not been,
>   And their children after them.
>   10. Nevertheless, these were men of piety,
>   And their hope hath not ceased; [4]

---

[1] Verse 31 is wanting in *Heb*.
[2] The text of *Heb.* is mutilated.
[3] This title occurs in *Heb*.
[4] Or " been cut off "; the text of *Heb.* is mutilated.

11. With their seed their goodness remaineth sure,   **H.**
    And their inheritance to their children's
    children.
12. Their seed standeth fast in the covenants,   **G.**
    And in their children for their sakes;[1]
13. Their memory abideth for ever,   **H.**
    And their righteousness shall not be forgotten.
14. Their bodies were buried in peace,   **G.**
    But their name liveth unto all generations.[2]
15. The assembly repeateth their wisdom,   **H.**
    And the congregation declareth their praise.[3]

Enoch and Noah

16. Enoch was found perfect, and he walked with
    Jehovah, and was taken;
    A sign of knowledge to every generation.
17. Noah the righteous was found perfect,
    In the time of destruction he became the renewer;
    For his sake there was a remnant,
    And because of his covenant the Flood ceased;
18. An eternal covenant did [God] make with him
    Not to destroy all flesh [again].

Abraham, Isaac, and Jacob

19. Abraham, the father of a multitude of nations,
    Put no blemish on his honour;
20. He kept the commandments of the Most High,
    And entered into a covenant with Him;
    In his flesh he made a covenant with Him,
    And in temptation he was found faithful.
21. Wherefore, with an oath He established him,[4]
    To bless nations in his seed;
    To multiply him as the dust of the earth,[5]   **G.**
    And to exalt his seed as the stars;[5]

---

[1] Verse 12 is wanting in *Heb.*
[2] The text of *Heb.* is almost entirely obliterated.
[3] Verse 15 occurs only in the margin of *Heb.*
[4] *Syr.* reads: "sware unto him"; this is probably the force of the Hebrew here; the cognate Aramaic root means "to swear."
[5] These lines are omitted in *Heb.*

H.   To cause them to inherit from sea to sea,
    And from the River to the ends of the earth.
22. And also Isaac did He establish [1] likewise,
    For the sake of Abraham his father;
    The covenant of all his ancestry He gave him.
23.   And a blessing rested on the head of Israel;
    Yea, He established him with a blessing,[2]
    And gave him his inheritance;
    And He set him for tribes,
    To be divided into twelve.

Moses

    And He brought out from him a man of mercy,[3]
    Who found grace in the sight of all living.[3]
XLV. 1. Beloved of God and men
    Was Moses of happy memory.
2. And He made him glorious [4] as God,
    And made him mighty in awe-inspiring deeds.
G. 3. By his words he caused wonders to happen in
    quick succession,[5]
H.   And He made him bold in the presence of the
    king.
    And He gave him a charge unto the people,
    And showed him His glory.[6]
4. For his faithfulness and his meekness,
    He chose him out of all flesh,
5. And caused him to hear His voice,
    And let him draw nigh unto the dark cloud;
    And He placed in his hand the commandment,
    Even the Law of life and discernment;
    That he might teach statutes unto Jacob,
    And His testimonies and judgements unto Israel.

[1] See last note but one.
[2] *Heb.* margin reads: " And He gave him the title of First-born "; this is to be preferred.
[3] It is possible that the reference in these lines is to Joseph, cp. Gen. xxxix. 4, 21.
[4] The first word of this line in *Heb.* is mutilated.
[5] With the exception of the last word this line is almost wholly obliterated in *Heb.*
[6] The text of *Heb.* is mutilated.

Aaron

6. And He exalted a holy one like unto him,   **H.**
   Even Aaron of the tribe of Levi;
7. And made him an eternal ordinance,
   And bestowed upon him His majesty;
   And He blessed him with His glory,
   And girded him with beauteous magnificence.
8. And He clothed him with the perfection of
   adornment,
   And adorned him with splendid vestments,
   The breeches, the tunic, and the robe,
9. And encompassed him with pomegranates,
   And with resounding bells round about,
   To make music with his steps,
   So as to cause the sound of him to be heard in
   the inmost shrine,
   For a memorial for the children of his people;
10. [With] the holy garments of gold and violet,
   And purple, the work of the designer;
   And the breast-plate of judgement, and the
   ephod and waist-cloth;
11. And the scarlet, the work of the weaver,
   [With] precious stones seal-engraven,
   In settings, the work of the stone-engraver;[1]
   For a memorial in graven writing,
   According to the number of the tribes of Israel,
12. [With] a crown of pure gold upon [his] mitre,
   The diadem engraven " Holy to Jehovah,"[2]
   Glorious majesty and mighty praise,
   The desire of the eyes, goodly and beautiful.[3]   **G.**
13. Before him there never were such things,[3]
   Never did a stranger put them on[3];
   He trusted him and his sons only,[2]   **H.**
   And his son's sons throughout their generations.[2]
14. His meal-offering is wholly consumed
   Twice every day as a continual sacrifice.

[1] Reconstructed text; the line is almost wholly mutilated in *Heb.*
[2] Reconstructed text; *Heb.* is mutilated.
[3] The text of *Heb.* is much mutilated.

I

H. 15. Moses consecrated him,
  And anointed him with the holy oil;
  And it became for him an eternal covenant,
    And for his seed as the days of heaven;
  To minister and to execute the priest's office
      for Him,
    And to bless His people in His name.
  16. He chose him out of all living,
    To bring near the burnt-offerings and the fat
        pieces,
  And to burn a sweet savour and a memorial,
    And to make atonement for the children of
        Israel.
  17. And He gave them His commandments,
    And invested him with authority over statute
        and judgement,
  That he might teach His people statutes,
    And judgements unto the children of Israel.
  18. But strangers were incensed against him,
    And were envious against him in the wilderness;
  The men of Dathan and Abiram,
    And the company of Korah in the violence of
        their wrath.
  19. And Jehovah saw it and was angered,
    And consumed them in His fierce wrath;
  And He brought to pass a sign upon them,
    And devoured them with His fiery flame.
  20. And He increased his glory unto Aaron,
    And gave him his inheritance:
  The holy contributions for their sustenance,
21a.   The fire-offerings of Jehovah they might eat,
20d. The bread of the presence [1] is his portion,
21b.   And the gift-sacrifice for him and for his seed.
  22. Only in the land of the people [1] might he have
        no heritage,
    And in their midst divide no inheritance;
  Whose portion and inheritance is Jehovah,[1]
    In the midst of the children of Israel.

        [1] Reconstructed text; *Heb.* is mutilated,

Phinehas

23. Moreover, Phinehas, the son of Eleazar,   **H.**
    Was glorious in might as a third,[1]
    In that he was jealous for the God of all,
    And stood in the breach for his people;
    While his heart prompted him,
    And he made atonement for the children of
    Israel.
24. Therefore also for him He established an ordi-
    nance,
    A covenant of peace to maintain the sanctuary;
    That to him and to his seed should appertain
    The High-Priesthood for ever.
25. And also with David was his covenant,
    The son of Jesse, of the tribe of Judah;
    The inheritance of the king is his son's alone,[2]
    While the inheritance of Aaron [belongs] to
    him, and to his seed.
    And now bless ye Jehovah, the Good,
    Who hath crowned you with honour;
26. May He grant you wisdom of heart,
    To judge His people in righteousness,[3]   **G.**
    That your prosperity may never cease,   **H.**
    Nor your power for eternal generations.

Joshua and Caleb

XLVI. 1. A mighty man of valour was Joshua, the
    son of Nun,
    A minister of Moses in the prophetical office,
    Who was created to be according to his name,[4]
    A great salvation for His chosen ones,
    To take vengeance upon the enemy,
    And to give an inheritance to Israel.
2. How glorious was he when he stretched forth his
    hand,
    And brandished his javelin against the city!

---

[1] Reconstructed text; *Heb.* is mutilated.
[2] Reconstructed text; *Heb.* is corrupt.
[3] This line is wanting in *Heb.*
[4] Reconstructed text.

H. 3. Who was he [that was able] to stand before him
       When he fought the wars of Jehovah?
    4. Was it not by his hand that the sun stood still
       And one day became as two? [1]
    5. For he called unto God Most High,
       When he was in sore straits, [and] his enemies
          around him,[1]
       And God Most High answered him,
       With hailstones and bolts; [1]
    6. He cast them down upon the hostile people.[1]
       And in the going down he destroyed them that
          rose up,[1]
       That all the nations [devoted to] destruction
          might know
       That Jehovah was watching their fighting;
       And also because he fully followed after God,
    7.   And did an act of piety in the days of Moses,
       He and Caleb, the son of Jephunneh,
          In standing firm when the congregation broke
             loose,
       To turn away wrath from the assembly,
       And to cause the evil report to cease.
    8. Wherefore also they two were set apart,
       From among the six hundred thousand footmen,
       To bring them into their inheritance,
       [Into] a land flowing with milk and honey.
    9. And He gave strength unto Caleb,
       And unto old age it stood by him,
       To cause him to tread upon the high places of the
          land;
       And also his seed obtained a heritage,
   10. That all the seed of Jacob might know
       That it is good to follow wholly after Jehovah.

The Judges

   11. Also the Judges, each with his name,
       All whose hearts were not beguiled,
       Nor turned back from [following] after God,
       Let their memory be for a blessing.

          [1] Reconstructed text.

12. May their bones flourish again out of their place,[1] G.
　　And may their name sprout afresh for [2] their H.
　　children.

Samuel

13. Honoured by his people, and loved by his Maker
　　[Was] " He that was asked " [3] from his mother's
　　womb;
　　Sanctified in the prophetical office by Jehovah,
　　Samuel, [who acted as] judge and priest.
　　By the word of God he established the kingdom,
　　And anointed princes over the people.
14. By means of the commandment he commanded
　　the congregation,
　　And he visited the gods [4] of Jacob.
15. By his faithfulness he was proved to be a prophet,[5] G.
　　And by his word a faithful seer.　　　　　　　 H.
16. And when his enemies pressed him on every side,[5] G.
　　He called upon the Lord, the Mighty One,[5]
　　With the offering of a sucking lamb.[5]
17. And the Lord thundered from heaven; [5]
　　With a mighty crash His voice was heard,　　 H.
18. And He subdued the strong places of the enemy,
　　And destroyed all the princes of the Philistines.
19. And at the time when he rested upon his bed,
　　He called Jehovah and His anointed to witness :
　　" From whom have I taken a bribe, or a pair
　　of shoes ? " [6]
　　And no man accused him.
　　And also to the time of his end he was found
　　upright
　　In the eyes of Jehovah, and in the eyes of all
　　living.

[1] This line is wanting in *Heb.*; but see xlix. 10 for the
idea.
[2] Or " as regards," *i. e.* in.
[3] In *Heb.* a word-play on " Samuel."
[4] This is a corruption; read " tents."
[5] The text of *Heb.* is much mutilated.
[6] See 1 Sam. xii. 3 in the Septuagint, which is followed
both here and in *Grk.*

H. 20. And even after his death he was enquired of,
       And he declared to the king his fate;[1]
       And he lifted his voice from the earth,
G.   To blot out the wickedness of the people.[2]

David

H. XLVII. 1. And, furthermore, after him stood up
       Nathan,
       To stand in the presence of David;
   2. For as the fat is separated [3] from the offering,
       So was David [separated] from Israel.
   3. He played with lions as with kids,
       And with bears as with calves of Bashan.
   4. In his youth he slew the giant,
       And took away the reproach from the people;
       When he slung his hand with the sling,
       And broke the pride of Goliath.
   5. For he called unto God Most High.
       And He gave strength to his right hand,
       That it might strike down the man experienced
       in wars,
       And that he might lift up the horn of his people.
   6. Therefore the daughters sang of him,
       And honoured him, [the slayer of] ten thousand.
       When he had put on the diadem he fought,
   7.   And subdued the enemy round about,
       And he put cities among the Philistines,[4]
       And brake in pieces their power [5] unto this day.
   8. In all his doings he gave thanks
       Unto God Most High with words of glory;
       With his whole heart he loved his Maker,
G.   And sang praise every day continually.[6]
H. 9. Stringed instruments and song before the altar
       [he ordained],[7]

---

[1] *Lit.* "way."
[2] In *Heb.* only one word of this line, "in the prophetical
office," is left.   [3] *Lit.* "lifted up."
[4] The text of the line is corrupt; we should perhaps read :
"And he destroyed the cities of the Philistines."
[5] *Lit.* "horn."   [6] Reconstructed text.
[7] This is added in the margin of *Heb.*

To make sweet melody with their music.[1]   G.
10. He gave comeliness to the feasts,[1]
   And set in order the seasons to perfection,[1]
   While they praised His holy name;   H.
   Before morning it resounded from the sanctuary.
11. Moreover, Jehovah put away his transgression,
   And lifted up his horn for ever.
   And He gave him the decree of the kingdom,
   And established his throne over Israel.

Solomon

12. And for his sake there stood up after him
   A wise son dwelling in safety.
13. Solomon reigned in days of peace,
   And God gave him rest round about.
   He prepared a house for His name,
   And established a sanctuary for ever.
14. How wise wast thou in thy youth,
   And overflowedst, like the Nile, with instruc-
      tion;
15. Thou didst cover the earth with thy soul,[2]
   And didst gather songs in the height.[3]
16. Thy name reached unto the isles afar off;   G.
   And for thy peace thou wast beloved.[4]
17. By thy songs, parables, dark speeches,   H.
   And satires thou didst astonish the peoples.
18. Thou wast called by the glorious name,
   Which is called over Israel.
   Thou didst heap up gold like tin,
   And didst multiply silver like lead.
19. But thou gavest thy loins unto women,
   And didst cause them to rule over thy body;
20. Yea, thou broughtest a blemish upon thine
      honour,
   And didst defile thy bed,

---

[1] The text of *Heb.* is for the most part obliterated.
[2] *I. e.* influence.
[3] The text of *Heb.* is corrupt; we should probably emend
so as to read : " And didst gather parables like the sea."
[4] Verse 16 is wanting in *Heb.*

H. So as to bring wrath upon thy progeny,
And sighing concerning thy couch.
21. So the people became two sceptres,
And from Ephraim [arose] a sinful kingdom.
22. Nevertheless, God did not forsake His mercy,[1]
And suffered not any of His words to fall to
the ground;
He will not cut off the posterity of His chosen,[1]
And the offspring of them that love Him He
will not destroy;
And He gave to Jacob a remnant,[1]
And to the house of David a root from him.[1]

Solomon's Successors

23. And Solomon slept in Jerusalem,[1]
And left after him one that was overbearing;[1]
Great in folly, and lacking in understanding
[Was] Rehoboam, who [2] by his counsel made
the people to revolt,
Until there arose—let there be no memorial of
him—Jeroboam the son of Nebat,[3]
Who sinned, and made Israel to sin;
And he put a stumbling-block [before] Ephraim,
24. To drive them from their land;
And their sin became very great,
And they sold themselves to do all manner of
evil.

Elijah

XLVIII. 1. Until there arose a prophet like fire,
And his word was like a burning furnace.
2. And he broke for them the staff of bread,
And by his zeal he made them small in number.
3. By the word of God he shut up the heavens,
Also fire came down three times.
4. How terrible wast thou, Elijah !
And he who is like thee shall be glorified.

---

[1] Reconstructed text.
[2] The text of *Heb.* is corrupt; we should probably read :
" he who."
[3] The text of *Heb.* is corrupt.

5. [Thou] who didst raise up a corpse from death,   **H.**
   And from Sheol by the favour of Jehovah;
6. Who broughtest down kings to the Pit,
   And them that were honoured from their beds
     [of sickness];
7. Who heardest rebukes from Sinai,
   And from Horeb judgements of vengeance.
8. Who anointed kings for retribution,
   And a prophet to succeed in thy place.
9. Who in the whirlwind wast taken upwards,
   And with fiery troops to the heavens.
10. Who art written as ready for the time,
   To still wrath before the fierce anger of God,
   To turn the hearts of the fathers unto the
     children,
   And to restore the tribes of Israel.
11. Blessed is he that seeth thee, and dieth,
   And they that have been beautified with love.[1]   **G.**
   For we also shall surely live.[2]

Elisha

12. Elijah [it was] who was wrapped in a tempest,[3]
   Then was Elisha filled with his spirit.[3]
   In double measure did he multiply signs,   **H.**
   And wonderful was all that went forth from
     his mouth.
   [During] his days he moved before none,
   And no flesh ruled over his spirit;
13. Nothing was too wonderful for him,
   And from his grave [4] his flesh prophesied.
14. In his life he did wonderful acts,
   And in his death marvellous works.
15. For all this the people turned not,
   And ceased not from their sins;
   Until they were plucked from their land,
   And were scattered in all the earth;

---

[1] This line is almost wholly mutilated in *Heb.*
[2] This line is probably a later addition.
[3] The text of *Heb.* is almost wholly mutilated.
[4] *Lit.* " from beneath him."

H.   And there were left in Judah but a few;
          Yet to the house of David was left a prince.
16. Some of them did that which was right,
          And some of them did wondrous wickedly.

Hezekiah and Isaiah

17. Hezekiah fortified his city
          By bringing water into the midst of it;
        And he hewed the rocks with iron,
          And dammed up the pool with mountains.
18. In his days Sennacherib came up,
          And sent Rabshakeh,·
        Who stretched forth his hand against Zion,
          And blasphemed God in his pride.
19. Then were they shaken in the pride of their
          heart,
          And they writhed like a woman in travail;
20. So they called unto God Most High,
          And spread forth their hands unto Him,
        And He heard the voice of their prayer,
          And saved them by the hand of Isaiah.
21. And He smote the army of Assyria,
          And discomfited them by the plague.
G. 22. For Hezekiah did that which was pleasing unto
          the Lord,[1]
H.   And was strong in the ways of David,
G.   Which Isaiah the prophet commanded,[2]
          Who was great and faithful in his vision.[2]
23. In his days the sun went backward,[2]
          And he added life to the king.[2]
24. By a spirit of might he saw the latter end,
          And comforted the mourners of Zion.
25. Unto eternity he declared the things that shall
          be,
          And hidden things before they came to
          pass.[3]

---

[1] The text of *Heb.* is much mutilated.
[2] The text of *Heb.* is entirely obliterated.
[3] See *The Martyrdom of Isaiah*, chap. iv.

Josiah

XLIX. 1. The name of Josiah is as sweet-smelling **G**
  incense,
  That is well mixed, the work of the apothecary.
  The memorial of him is sweet in the palate like **H.**
  honey,
  And as music at a banquet of wine.
2. For he was grieved at their backslidings,
  And caused the vain abominations to cease;
3. And he gave his heart wholly to God,
  And in days of violence he practised piety.

Jeremiah

4. Excepting David, Hezekiah,
  And Josiah, they all dealt corruptly,
  And forsook the Law of the Most High,—
  The kings of Judah, until their end.
5. And their might [1] was given to others,
  And their glory to a strange nation.
6. And so the Holy City was burned,
  And the ways thereof laid waste,
  Through Jeremiah, 7. because they persecuted
  him,
  And he a prophet from the womb,
  " To pluck up, to break down, and to destroy,
  And likewise to build, and to plant," [2] and to
  strengthen.

Ezekiel, Job, and the Twelve Prophets

8. Ezekiel saw a vision,
  And declared the different beings of the chariot.
9. He also made mention of Job among the prophets, [3]
  Who was complete in all the ways of righteous-
  ness.
10. And also the Twelve Prophets,
  May their bones sprout beneath them, [4]
  Who made Jacob whole,
  And delivered him by confident hope? [3]

[1] *Lit.* " horn."   [2] See Jer. i. 10.
[3] Emended text.   [4] Cf. xlvi. 12.

Zerubbabel, Joshua, Nehemiah

G. 11. How shall we magnify Zerubbabel,[1]
      He, indeed, was a signet on the right hand; [1]
   12. And also Jesus, the son of Josedek? [1]
      Who in their days built the House,[1]
H.   And set up on high the Holy Temple,
      Which was prepared for everlasting glory.
   13. Nehemiah,—glorious is his memory !
      Who raised up our ruins,
      And healed our breaches,
      And set up gates and bars.

The Patriarchs

   14. Few have been created on the earth like Enoch;
      He also was taken up from off the face thereof.[2]
   15*a*. Like Joseph was ever a man born ?
   15*c*.   His body also was visited.[3]
   16. Shem, and Seth, with Enoch were visited; [4]
      But above every living thing was the glory of
      Adam.

Simeon, the son of Jochanan

   15*b*. Great among his brethren, and the glory of his
      people
L. 1. Was Simeon, the son of Jochanan, the priest.
      In whose time [5] the house was renovated,   .
      And in whose days the Temple was fortified;
   3. In whose time [5] a reservoir was dug,
      A water-cistern like the sea in abundance.
   2. In his days the wall was built,
      [With] turrets for strength like a king's palace.
   4. He took thought for his people [protecting them]
      from spoliation,
      And fortified his city against the enemy.

[1] The text of *Heb.* is almost entirely obliterated.
[2] Emended text.
[3] See Gen. l. 25; Exod. xiii. 19; Josh. xxiv. 32.
[4] The text of *Heb.* is corrupt; we should probably read :
" honoured."
[5] *Lit.* " generation."

5. How glorious was he when he looked forth from **H.**
     the Tent,
     And when he came out of the sanctuary.[1]
6. Like a morning star [2] from between the clouds,
     And like the full moon on the feast-days,
7. Like the sun shining upon the Temple of the
     King,
     And like the bow appearing in the cloud;
8. Like blossoms on a branch in the days of first-
     fruits,[3]
     And as a lily by the water-brooks,
   As the sprout of Lebanon in the days of summer,
9.   And as the fire of incense in the censer;
     Like a golden vessel beautifully wrought,[4]
     Adorned with all manner of precious stones;
10. Like a luxuriant olive-tree full of berries,
     And like an oleaster nourishing branches.
11. When he put on his glorious robes,
     And clothed himself in full splendour,
     When he went up to the altar of majesty,
     And made glorious the court of the sanctuary;
12. When he took the portions from the hands of
     his brethren,
     And he standing by the prepared wood,
   Around him [was] the garland [5] of his sons,
     Like young cedar-trees in Lebanon;
   And like willows by the brook did they surround
     him;
13.   All the sons of Aaron in their glory,
   And the fire-offering of Jehovah in their hand,
     In the presence of all the congregations of
     Israel.
14. Until he had finished the service of the altar;
     And setting in order the rows of wood for the
     Most High,

---

[1] *Lit.* " the house of atonement."
[2] *Lit.* " star of the light."
[3] Emended text.
[4] The text of *Heb.* is uncertain.
[5] *Lit.* " crown."

G. 15. He stretched his hand to the cup,[1]
    And poured out the blood of the grape,[1]
    Yea, he poured it out at the foot of the altar,[1]
    A sweet-smelling savour unto the Most High,
      the King of all.[1]

H. 16. Then sounded the sons of Aaron
    With the trumpets of beaten work;
    Yea, they sounded, and caused a mighty blast [2]
      to be heard,
    For a remembrance before the Most High.

17. [Then] all flesh hasted together,
    And fell upon their faces to the earth,
    To worship before the Most High,
    Before the Holy One of Israel;

18. And the song then gave its voice,
    And over the multitude they arranged its
      lamp; [3]

19. And all the people of the land cried
    In prayer before the Merciful,
    Until he had finished the service of the altar,
    And His ordinances had brought him nigh unto
      Him.

20. Then he came down and lifted up his hands
    Upon all the congregation of Israel,
    And the blessing of Jehovah [was] upon his lips,
    And in the name of Jehovah he glorified himself.

21. And a second time they fell down, [now] to receive
    The pardon of God from him.[4]

22. Now bless the God of all,
    Who doeth wondrously on earth,
    Who exalteth man from the womb,
    And doeth unto him according. to His good
      pleasure.

23. May He grant unto you wisdom of heart,
    And may there be peace among you.

---

[1] These lines have been accidentally omitted in *Heb.*
[2] *Lit.* " voice."
[3] The text of *Heb.* is corrupt; we should probably read ;
" they made sweet melody."
[4] Emended text; *Heb.* is mutilated.

24. May His mercy be established with Simeon,   **H.**
      And may He raise up for him the covenant of
        Phinehas;
    May there not be one cut off from him,
      And as to his seed [may it be] as the days of
        heaven.

L. 25, 26. **Three Detested Nations**

25. Against two nations doth my soul feel abhorrence,
      And [against] a third, [which is] not a people :
26. The inhabitants of Seir, and Philistia,
      And that foolish nation which dwelleth in
        Sichem.

L. 27–29. **Subscription to the Book**

27. Wise instruction and apt proverbs
      Of Simeon, the son of Jeshua, the son of Eleazar,
        the son of Sira,
    Which he declared in the explanation of his
      heart,[1]
    And which he taught with his understanding.
28. Blessed is the man who meditateth on these
      things;
      And he that layeth them up in his heart shall
        become wise.
29. For if he do them, he shall be strong for all **G.**
      things,[2]
      For the fear of Jehovah is life.   **H.**

LI. 1–30. **Appendix to the Book**

A Prayer

1. I will thank Thee, Jehovah, O King,
      I will praise Thee, O God of my salvation;
    I will declare Thy name, Thou strength of my
      life;
2.   For Thou hast redeemed my soul from death,
    Thou hast kept back my flesh from the Pit,

---

[1] Emended text.
[2] This line has been accidentally omitted in *Heb.*

H. And hast delivered my feet from the hand of
Sheol.

Thou didst preserve me from the slander of the
people, from the scourge of a slanderous
tongue,

And from the lips of those who turn aside to
lying,

Thou wast with me in the presence of those who
rose up against me.

3.   Thou didst help me, according to the abundance
of Thy mercy,

Out of the snare of those watching for my down-
fall,[1]

And from the hand of those that seek my
life;

Out of many troubles hast Thou saved me,

4.   And from the straits of the flame [round about
me],

From the midst of the fire that I kindled not,[1]

5.   From the deep of the belly of Sheol,[2]

From wickedly devising lips, and from them that
plaster falsehood,

6.   And [from] the arrows of a deceitful tongue.
My soul drew nigh unto death,

And my life to the nethermost Sheol;

7. And I turned about on every side, and there was
none that helped me;

Yea, I looked for one to uphold, but there was
none.

8. Then I remembered the lovingkindnesses of
Jehovah,

And His mercies which have been from of old;

He delivereth them that put their trust in Him,

And redeemeth them from all evil.

9. And I lifted up my voice from the earth,

And from the gates of Sheol I cried;

10. Yea, I cried:[3] "Jehovah, my Father art Thou,

My God, and the strength[4] of my salvation,

---

[1] Emended text.
[2] Following *Grk.*; the text of *Heb.* is corrupt.
[3] Emended text.   [4] *Lit.* "the hero."

Forsake me not in the day of trouble,   **H.**
  In the day of wasteness and desolation. [1]

11. I will praise Thy name continually,
  And will remember Thee in prayer."
Then did Jehovah hear my voice,
  And gave ear to my supplication.

12. And He redeemed from all evil,
  And delivered me in the day of trouble;
Therefore will I give thanks [unto Him] and
    praise [Him],
  And I will bless the name of Jehovah :

A Thanksgiving [2]

i. Give thanks unto Jehovah, for He is good,
  For His mercy endureth for ever.

ii. Give thanks to the God of praises,
  For His mercy endureth for ever.

iii. Give thanks unto the Keeper of Israel,
  For His mercy endureth for ever.

iv. Give thanks unto the Framer of all,
  For His mercy endureth for ever.

v. Give thanks unto the Redeemer of Israel,
  For His mercy endureth for ever.

vi. Give thanks unto Him that gathereth the out-
    casts of Israel,
  For His mercy endureth for ever.

vii. Give thanks unto Him that buildeth His City
    and His Sanctuary,
  For His mercy endureth for ever.

viii. Give thanks unto Him that causeth a horn to
    sprout for the house of David,
  For His mercy endureth for ever.

ix. Give thanks unto Him that chooseth the sons of
    Zadok for priests,
  For His mercy endureth for ever.

x. Give thanks unto the Shield of Abraham,
  For His mercy endureth for ever.

xi. Give thanks unto the Rock of Isaac,
  For His mercy endureth for ever.

[1] Quoted from Zeph. i. 15.
[2] This thanksgiving only occurs in *Heb*.

K

H. xii. Give thanks unto the Mighty One of Jacob,
   For His mercy endureth for ever.
 xiii. Give thanks unto Him that chooseth Zion,
   For His mercy endureth for ever.
 xiv. Give thanks unto the King of the Kings of Kings,
   For His mercy endureth for ever.
 xv. And He hath exalted the horn of His people,
   The praise of all His pious ones,
 xvi. For the children of Israel, a people nigh unto
   Him ;
   Hallelujah.

A Poem

 13. I was a youth [1]
   When I desired her and sought her out.
 14. In my youth I made supplication and prayer,
G. And I will seek her out even unto the end.[2]
 15. She blossomed like a ripening grape,[3]
   My heart rejoiced in her ; [4]
H. My foot trod in her footstep ;
   From my youth I learned Wisdom.
G. 16. I bowed down mine ear a little and received her,[5]
H. And much knowledge I found.
 17. And her yoke was a glory unto me ;
   And to my Teacher do I offer thanks.
 18. I purposed to do good,[6]
   And I will not turn back, for I will find her.
 19. My soul was attached to her,
   And my face I turned not away from her.
G. I spread forth my hands to the Heaven above,[5]
H. And for ever and ever I will not swerve from her.
  My hand opened her gates,
   And unto her I entered, and looked upon her.

---

[1] This line is too short; something has evidently fallen out; *Grk.* adds : " before I wandered abroad."
[2] This line is wanting in *Heb.*
[3] Emended text.
[4] The two first lines of verse 15 are missing in *Heb.*
[5] This line is missing in *Heb.*
[6] This line is too short; we should probably add : " with her," following *Grk.*

20. I directed my soul after her,   H.
    And in her purity I found her;
    I got me understanding [1] through her guidance,
    Therefore shall I not be forsaken.   G.
21. Mine inward parts were troubled like an oven H.
    [in my desire] to look upon her,
    Therefore I have gotten a good possession.
22. Jehovah gave me the reward of my lips,
    And with my tongue do I praise Him.
23. Turn in unto me, ye unlearned,
    And lodge in my house of instruction.
24. How long will ye lack these things,[2]
    And your soul be so sore athirst?
25. My mouth I open and speak of her,
    Get Wisdom for yourselves without money.
26. Bring your necks under her yoke,
    And her burden let your soul bear;
    She is nigh unto them that seek her,
    And he that yearneth [3] [for her] findeth her.
27. See with your eyes that but a short time I laboured
    for her,[4]
    And found abundance of peace.
28. Hearken unto my teaching in [however small] a
    number,
    And much silver and gold will ye acquire
    thereby.
29. May my soul delight in my Yeshibah,[5]
    And ye shall not be ashamed to sing my praise.
30. Work your work before the time,[6]
    And He will give you your reward in its time.

Blessed be Jehovah, and praised be His name to
generations.

[1] *Lit.* " heart."
[2] *Lit.* " from these things and those things."
[3] *Lit.* " giveth his soul."
[4] Emended text.
[5] *I. e.* an academy of learning.
[6] *I. e.* the time of the end; the text is emended on the
basis of *Grk.*

Subscription

Thus far the words of Simeon, the son of Jeshua, that is called Ben-Sira.

The Wisdom of Simeon, the son of Jeshua, the son of Eleazar, the son of Sira.

May the name of Jehovah be blessed from now even unto eternity.

PRINTED IN GREAT BRITAIN BY RICHARD CLAY & SONS, LIMITED.
BRUNSWICK ST., STAMFORD ST., S.E., AND BUNGAY, SUFFOLK.

CPSIA information can be obtained
at www.ICGtesting.com
Printed in the USA
LVHW080200100920
665506LV00010B/85